BITCOIN AND CRYPTOCURRENCY TRADING FOR BEGINNERS

The Ultimate Guide on How to Invest and Trade in Crypto. Learn Easly Basic Definitions, Crypto Exchanges and Right Investment Advanced Strategy to Make a Passive Income.

2 books in 1

Mattehw Bickers

© Copyright 2021 by

The purpose of this document is to provide accurate and reliable information on the subject and problem at hand. The book is sold to understand that the publisher is not obligated to provide accounting, legally authorized, or otherwise eligible services. If legal or professional advice is needed, a well-versed professional should be consulted.

A Committee of the American Bar Association and a Committee of Publishers and Associations also adopted and endorsed the Declaration of Principles.

The data presented here is said to be accurate and reliable. Any liability arising from the use or misuse of any procedures, processes, or instructions contained herein, whether due to inattention or otherwise, is solely and completely the responsibility of the recipient reader. Under no conditions will the publisher be held liable for any reparation, damages, or monetary loss incurred due to the information contained herein, whether directly or indirectly.

The knowledge provided here is strictly for educational purposes and is therefore universal. The information is presented without some kind of contract or guarantee assurance.

The trademarks are used without the trademark owner's permission or backing, and the trademark is published without the trademark owner's permission or backing. All trademarks and labels mentioned in this book are their respective owners' property and are not associated with this.

TABLE OF CONTENTS

2 books in 1

CRYPTOCURRENCY TRADING FOR BEGINNERS

BITCOIN TRADING FOR BEGINNERS

INTRODUCTION

Cryptocurrencies, also known as virtual currencies, are digital forms of trade that are secured through cryptography. The term "crypto" comes from the Greek word "kryptós," which means "secret" or "personal." There are several advantages to a digital currency that is developed and used by private individuals or organizations.

Cryptocurrency is electronic money created with technology that controls its development and protects transactions while concealing its users' identities. Cryptography is a type of computer technology used for encryption, hiding information, and establishing identities. Currency simply means "actually used currency.

Cryptocurrencies are a form of digital money designed to be faster, cheaper, and more dependable than traditional government-issued currency. Rather than relying on the government to produce the money and banks to store, send, and receive it, users transact directly with one another and store their funds. Transactions are typically very cheap and fast since people can submit money directly without going through a middleman.

To avoid fraud and corruption, each cryptocurrency user can record and verify their transactions and other users' transactions simultaneously. The digital transaction records are referred to as a "ledger," which is open to the public. Transactions become more effective, permanent, stable, and transparent with this public ledger.

Cryptocurrencies do not ask you to trust a bank to keep your money because of public records. They don't need you to have faith in the person with whom you're doing business to pay you. Instead, thousands of people will see the money being sent, collected, checked, and registered. There is no need for confidence in this scheme. This one-of-a-kind positive trait is referred to as "trustless.

CHAPTER 1: EVERYTHING YOU MUST KNOW ABOUT CRYPTOCURRENCY

WHAT EXACTLY IS A CRYPTOCURRENCY?

A cryptocurrency (or crypto) is a type of digital money that allows people to send money over the internet.
You may be wondering how this method varies from PayPal or your smartphone's digital banking app. On the surface, they tend to serve the same purposes – paying friends, making transactions from your favorite website – but they couldn't be more dissimilar under the hood.

WHAT DISTINGUISHES CRYPTOCURRENCY FROM OTHER DIGITAL CURRENCIES?

Cryptocurrency is distinct for a variety of reasons. However, its main purpose is to act as an electronic cash system that any one party does not control.
Decentralized is a key feature of a good cryptocurrency. There is no way for a central bank or a group of users to change the rules without gaining consensus. Participants in the network (nodes) run software that links them to other participants to exchange information.
Networks that are centralized vs. decentralized networks.

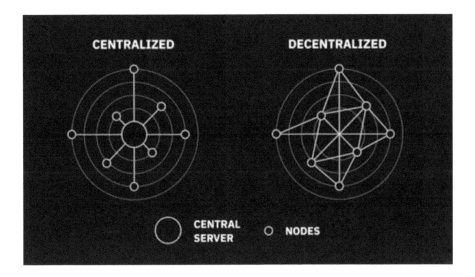

On the left, you'll find what you'd expect a bank to use. The central server is the only way for users to connect. There is no hierarchy on the right: nodes are interconnected and communicate with one another.

Cryptocurrency networks are extremely immune to censorship or shutdown due to their decentralization. A centralized network, on the other hand, can be crippled simply by disrupting the main server. It would be extremely difficult to ascertain users' balances if a bank's database was wiped clean with no backups.

Nodes hold a copy of the database in cryptocurrency. Each is essentially their server. Individual nodes can go offline, but their peers can still access data from other nodes.

As a result, cryptocurrencies are available 24 hours a day, 365 days a year. They allow the transfer of value without the use of intermediaries anywhere on the planet. This is why they're sometimes referred to as permissionless: they allow anyone with an Internet connection to send money.

WHAT IS THE MEANING OF THE TERM "CRYPTOCURRENCY"?

The word "cryptocurrency" is a combination of the terms "cryptography" and "currency." This is because cryptocurrency relies heavily on cryptographic techniques to protect user transactions.

WHAT IS PUBLIC-KEY CRYPTOGRAPHY, AND HOW DOES IT WORK?

The foundation of cryptocurrency networks is public-key cryptography. Users depend on it to send and receive money.

You have a public key and a private key in a public-key cryptography scheme. A private key is a very large number that no one could guess. It's often difficult to comprehend just how large this number is.

Guessing the outcome of 256 coin tosses is just as likely as guessing a private key in Bitcoin. You wouldn't be able to crack someone's key with today's machines until the world died of heat.

In either case, as the name implies, you must keep your private key private. You can, however, create a public key from this one. The public one can be given to anyone without risk. It's unlikely that they'll be able to reverse-engineer the public key to obtain the private key.

You can also sign data with your private key to generate digital signatures. It's similar to signing a contract in real life. The main difference is that anyone can determine if it is legitimate by comparing a signature to the corresponding public key. The user doesn't have to show their private key this way, but they can still prove they own it.

You can only invest your cryptocurrency funds if you have the corresponding private key. When you make a purchase, you're telling the network you'd like to pass your money around. This is stated in a message (i.e., transaction) signed and added to the cryptocurrency's database (the blockchain). To build a digital signature, you'll need your private key, as previously mentioned. Since someone with access to the database can check the signature, they can verify that the transaction is correct.

WHO IS THE INVENTOR OF CRYPTOCURRENCY?

There have been a few attempts at digital cash schemes over the years, but Bitcoin, which was launched in 2009, was the first of the cryptocurrencies. It was created under the pseudonym Satoshi

Nakamoto by an individual or group of people. Their true identity has remained a mystery to this day.

Bitcoin spawned a slew of new cryptocurrencies, some attempting to compete and others attempting to incorporate features not found in Bitcoin. Many blockchains now enable users to run decentralized applications using smart contracts in addition to sending and receiving funds. Ethereum is probably the most well-known blockchain example.

WHAT'S THE DIFFERENCE BETWEEN TOKENS AND CRYPTOCURRENCIES?

Cryptocurrencies and tokens tend to be the same at first glance. Both can be sent between blockchain addresses and are exchanged on exchanges.

Cryptocurrencies exist solely to serve as currency, whether as a medium of trade, a store of value, or a combination of the two. Each unit is functionally fungible, which means that one coin is equal to another in terms of value.

While Bitcoin and other early cryptocurrencies were intended to be used as money, later blockchains tried to do more. Ethereum, for example, is more than just a digital currency. Developers will use it to run code (smart contracts) on a distributed network and build tokens for several decentralized applications.

Tokens are similar to cryptocurrencies in that they can be used in the same way, but they are more versatile. You may make millions of similar ones or a small number with special characteristics. They can be anything from digital receipts to reward points, and they can be used to indicate a stake in a business.

The base currency (used to pay for purchases or applications) is different from the tokens on a smart-contract-capable protocol. The native currency of Ethereum, for example, is ether (ETH), which must be used to generate and pass tokens within the Ethereum network. The ERC-20 and ERC-721 specifications are used to create these tokens.

WHAT EXACTLY IS A CRYPTOCURRENCY WALLET?

A cryptocurrency wallet is essentially a storage device for your private keys. It may be a custom-built computer (hardware wallet), a P.C. or smartphone program, or even a paper piece.

The most common way for users to interact with a cryptocurrency network is through wallets. Different forms may have different functions – a paper wallet, for example, cannot sign transactions or display current fiat currency rates.

Software wallets (such as Trust Wallet) are used for day-to-day payments due to their simplicity. Hardware wallets are practically unrivaled in their ability to keep private keys safe from prying eyes in terms of security. Cryptocurrency users often use both forms of wallets to store their funds.

WHAT ARE CRYPTOCURRENCIES AND HOW DO THEY WORK?

The source codes and technical controls that support and secure cryptocurrencies are extremely difficult to understand. On the other hand, ordinary citizens are more than capable of grasping the fundamental principles and being knowledgeable cryptocurrency consumers.

Most cryptocurrencies are functional variants of Bitcoin, the first commonly utilized cryptocurrency. Cryptocurrencies, like standard currencies, convey value in units – for example, you might say, "I have 2.5 Bitcoin," just as you would say, "I have $2.50."

Several principles govern the meaning, protection, and legitimacy of cryptocurrencies.

WALLETS

Users of cryptocurrency have "wallets" that contain unique information that identifies them as the temporary owners of their devices. Wallets reduce the possibility of fraud for units that aren't being used, while private keys validate a cryptocurrency transaction's validity. Cryptocurrency exchange wallets are very vulnerable to hacking. For example, Mt. Gox, a Bitcoin exchange based in Japan, shut down and declared bankruptcy a few years ago after hackers systematically robbed it of more than $450 million in Bitcoin traded on its servers.

Wallets can be saved in the cloud, on an internal hard drive, or an external hard drive. At least one backup is highly recommended, regardless of how a wallet is kept. It's important to note that backing up a wallet just copies the record of a wallet's life and current ownership, not the individual cryptocurrency units.

BLOCKCHAIN

The blockchain (also known as "
blockchain") of a cryptocurrency is the master ledger that records and stores all previous transactions and operations, validating ownership of all units of the currency at any given time. A blockchain has a finite length – containing a finite number of transactions – that grows over time as a record of a cryptocurrency's entire transaction history to date.

Every node of the cryptocurrency's software network – the network of decentralized server farms operated by computer-savvy individuals or groups of individuals known as miners who continuously record and authenticate cryptocurrency transactions – stores identical copies of the blockchain.

A cryptocurrency transaction isn't complete before it's added to the blockchain, which happens in seconds. The transaction is normally permanent until it is completed. Unlike conventional payment providers such as PayPal and credit cards, most cryptocurrencies lack built-in refund or chargeback functions, though some newer cryptocurrencies may have rudimentary refund features.

The units aren't available for use by any party during the transaction's initiation and completion. Instead, they're kept in a kind of escrow – or, to put it another way, limbo. Double-spending, or the manipulation of cryptocurrency code to enable the same currency units to be duplicated and sent to multiple recipients, is thus prevented by the blockchain.

PRIVATE KEYS

Every cryptocurrency owner has a private key that verifies their identity and enables them to trade units. Users may generate their private keys, which are whole numbers between 1 and 78 digits long or use a random number generator. They can obtain and spend cryptocurrency once they have a key. The holder cannot invest or convert their cryptocurrency without the key, making their holdings useless before the key is retrieved.

Although this is an important security feature that helps prevent fraud and unauthorized use, it is also very strict. Tossing a wad of cash into a garbage incinerator is the digital equivalent of losing your private key. You can build a new private key and start accumulating cryptocurrency again, but you won't be able to recover the cryptocurrency held in your old, lost key. As a result, savvy cryptocurrency users are maniacally protective of their private keys, storing them in various digital (though usually not Internet-connected) and analog (i.e., paper) locations.

MINERS

Miners are the record-keepers and indirect judges of the worth of cryptocurrency societies. Miners use highly technological methods to check the completeness, consistency, and security of currencies' blockchains by using massive computing power quantities, mostly embodied in private server farms operated by mining collectives consisting of thousands of individuals. The procedure is similar in complexity to the quest for new prime numbers and often necessitates massive computational power quantities.

Miners' work generates new blockchain copies regularly, inserting recent, previously unverified transactions that haven't been included in any previous blockchain copy, effectively completing those transactions. Any addition is referred to as a block. All transactions that have occurred after the last new copy of the blockchain have been generated are in blocks.

The word "miners" refers to the fact that miners' efforts result in new cryptocurrency units. In reality, every newly generated blockchain copy comes with a two-part monetary reward: a fixed number of newly minted ("mined") cryptocurrency units and a variable number of existing units obtained from optional transaction fees charged by buyers (typically less than 1% of the transaction value).

Notable: Cryptocurrency mining used to be a potentially lucrative side business for those with the financial means to invest in power and hardware-intensive mining operations. Hobbyists without thousands of dollars can no longer afford to invest in professional-grade mining equipment. If you're looking for a way to supplement your daily salary, there are plenty of freelance opportunities that will pay you more.

Though sellers aren't charged transaction fees, miners can give fee-loaded transactions priority over fee-free transactions when developing new blockchains, even if the fee-free transactions came first in time. This encourages sellers to charge transaction fees because it allows them to get paid quicker, and as a result, transaction fees are fairly normal. Although it is technically possible for a new blockchain copy to be completely fee-free, this rarely happens in practice.

Cryptocurrencies automatically adapt to the amount of mining power operating to build new blockchain copies through instructions in their source codes – copies become more difficult to create as mining power increases and easier to create as mining power decreases. The aim is to maintain a pre-determined average period between new blockchain creations. For example, Bitcoin's is 10 minutes

Even though mining creates new cryptocurrency units regularly, most cryptocurrencies are built to have a finite supply – a main guarantor of value. In general, this means that as time passes, miners obtain fewer new units per new blockchain. Miners will eventually be paid only transaction fees for their jobs, but this has yet to be implemented in practice and could take some time. Observers estimate that the last Bitcoin unit will be mined sometime in the mid-22nd century, which isn't exactly around the corner if current trends continue.

Cryptocurrencies with finite supply are thus more akin to precious metals like gold than fiat currencies, which technically have a limitless supply.

CHAPTER 2: CRYPTOCURRENCY EXCHANGES

Many lesser-known cryptocurrencies can only be traded through private, peer-to-peer transactions, making them less liquid and difficult to value than other cryptocurrencies and fiat currencies.

Common cryptocurrencies, such as Bitcoin and Ripple, are traded on secondary exchanges close to forex markets for fiat currencies. (One example is the now-defunct Mt. Gox.) These platforms allow cryptocurrency holders to exchange their holdings for major fiat currencies like the U.S. dollar and euro and other cryptocurrencies (including less-popular currencies). They take a small percentage of each transaction's value in exchange for their services – typically less than 1%.

Cryptocurrency exchanges are essential for establishing liquid markets for popular cryptocurrencies and determining their value compared to conventional currencies. Exchange pricing, on the other hand, can be highly unpredictable. Following Mt. Gox's demise, bitcoin's U.S. dollar exchange rate plummeted by more than 50%, only to more than tenfold in 2017 as cryptocurrency demand exploded. You can also trade cryptocurrency futures on some cryptocurrency exchanges or monitor broad-based cryptocurrency portfolios in crypto indexes. This BBOD trader's testimonial goes into greater depth about cryptocurrency trading.

THE EVOLUTION OF CRYPTOCURRENCY

Far before the first digital alternative currencies appeared, cryptocurrency existed as a theoretical construct. Early cryptocurrency supporters shared the intention of using cutting-edge mathematical and computer science concepts to address what they saw as "traditional" fiat currencies' functional and political flaws.

TECHNICAL FOUNDATIONS

The scientific foundations of cryptocurrency can be traced back to the early 1980s, when an American cryptographer named David Chaum developed a "blinding" algorithm used in modern web-based encryption. The algorithm enabled parties to exchange stable, unalterable information, laying the groundwork for future electronic currency transfers. This was referred to as "blinded capital."

Chaum enlisted a few other cryptocurrency enthusiasts in the late 1980s to commercialize the idea of blinded money. After relocating to the Netherlands, he formed DigiCash, a for-profit company that created currency units based on the blinding algorithm. DigiCash's power was not decentralized, unlike Bitcoin and most other modern cryptocurrencies. Chaum's firm had a monopoly on supply management, equivalent to the monopoly on fiat currencies held by central banks.

DigiCash attempted to negotiate directly with individuals initially, but the Dutch central bank objected, and the proposal was shelved. DigiCash decided to sell only to approved banks in the face of a deadline, severely limiting its market potential. Later, Microsoft approached DigiCash about a potentially lucrative relationship that would have enabled early Windows users to make transactions in its currency. Still, the two companies couldn't agree, and DigiCash went out of business in the late 1990s.

Around the same time, Wei Dai, a renowned software developer, released a white paper on b-money. This virtual currency architecture included many of the fundamental features of modern cryptocurrencies, such as complex privacy security and decentralization. B-money, on the other hand, was never used as a medium of trade.

Shortly after, a Chaum associate named Nick Szabo created and published Bit Gold, a cryptocurrency that was notable for using blockchain technology, which is the most modern foundation of cryptocurrencies. Bit Gold, like DigiCash, never gained popularity and is no longer used as a medium of trade.

PRE-BITCOIN VIRTUAL CURRENCIES

Following DigiCash, much of the electronic financial transaction research and investment moved to more traditional, albeit digital, intermediaries like PayPal (itself a harbinger of mobile payment technologies that have exploded in popularity over the past ten years). In other parts of the world, DigiCash knockoffs such as Russia's WebMoney have sprung up.

E-gold was the most well-known virtual currency in the United States in the late 1990s and early 2000s. A Florida-based company called e-gold developed and controls the currency. The business, e-gold, was essentially a digital gold buyer. Customers, or consumers, sent their old jewelry, trinkets, and coins to e-warehouse gold's in exchange for digital "e-gold" – gold-denominated currency units. Users of e-gold may then swap their stocks with others, cash out for physical gold, or convert their e-gold into U.S. dollars.

E-gold had millions of active accounts and handled billions of dollars in transactions annually at its peak in the mid-2000s. Unfortunately, due to its weak security measures, e-gold has become a common target for hackers and phishing scammers, putting its users at risk of financial loss. By the mid-2000s, much of e-transaction gold's activity had become legally questionable, thanks to the company's lax legal enforcement procedures, which made it appealing to money laundering operations and small-scale Ponzi schemes. In the mid-and late-2000s, the site came under increasing legal scrutiny, and it eventually shut down in 2009.

THE MODERN CRYPTOCURRENCY BOOM AND BITCOIN

Bitcoin is commonly considered the first modern cryptocurrency since it was the first publicly used medium of exchange to combine decentralized power, user anonymity, blockchain-based record-keeping, and built-in scarcity. Satoshi Nakamoto, a pseudonymous individual or party, first proposed it in a white paper published in 2008.

In early 2009, Satoshi Nakamoto made Bitcoin available to the general public, and a small group of ardent supporters started trading and mining the currency. By late 2010, the first of dozens of similar cryptocurrencies – including common alternatives like Litecoin – had begun to emerge. Around the same time, the first public Bitcoin exchanges emerged.

WordPress became the first big retailer to accept Bitcoin payments in late 2012. Others followed suits, such as Newegg.com (an online electronics retailer), Expedia, and Microsoft. Hundreds of merchants now accept the world's most famous cryptocurrency as a valid form of payment. And new cryptocurrency applications sprout up at an alarming rate – Cryptomaniaks, for example, has a great look at the fast-growing world of cryptocurrency sports betting sites here.

Although few cryptocurrencies other than Bitcoin are commonly accepted for merchant payments, a growing number of active exchanges enable holders to exchange their cryptocurrencies for Bitcoin or fiat currencies, offering much-needed liquidity and flexibility. Since the late 2010s, big business and institutional investors have kept a close eye on what they refer to as the "crypto vacuum."

BENEFITS OF CRYPTOCURRENCY

Most cryptocurrencies are designed with scarcity in mind; the source code defines the maximum number of units that can ever exist. Cryptocurrencies are, therefore, more akin to precious metals than fiat currencies in this regard. They, like precious metals, provide inflation security that fiat currency users do not have.

Loosening of Government Currency Monopolies

Cryptocurrencies have a safe means of exchange independent of national banks such as the Federal Reserve of the United States and the European Central Bank. This appeals to those concerned that quantitative easing (central banks "printing currency" by buying government bonds) and other forms of loose monetary policy, such as near-zero interbank lending rates, would contribute to long-term economic uncertainty.

Many economists and political scientists believe that governments would eventually co-opt cryptocurrency, or at the very least, integrate aspects of cryptocurrency into fiat currencies (such as built-in scarcity and authentication protocols). This assuages some cryptocurrency supporters' concerns about fiat currencies' inflationary existence and physical cash's inherent instability.

Communities that are self-interested and self-policing

For cryptocurrencies, mining is built-in quality management and policing method. Miners have a financial interest in keeping reliable, up-to-date transaction records since they are compensated for their efforts. This ensures the credibility of the system and the currency's value.

Robust Privacy Protections

Early cryptocurrency advocates were concerned about privacy and anonymity, and they are still concerned today. Many cryptocurrency users use pseudonyms that are unrelated to any personal information, accounts, or stored data. While advanced community members can deduce users' identities, newer cryptocurrencies (post-Bitcoin) have additional safeguards that make it far more difficult.

Governments will find it more difficult to exact financial retribution.

When people of authoritarian countries fall foul of their governments, those governments can easily freeze or seize their domestic bank accounts and reverse local currency transactions. This is especially concerning in autocratic countries like China and Russia, where wealthy individuals who fall foul of the ruling party often face severe financial and legal problems with questionable origins.

Cryptocurrencies, unlike central bank-backed fiat currencies, are practically resistant to authoritarian caprice. State regulation – also considering international collaboration – is extremely unrealistic since cryptocurrency assets and transaction records are held in several locations across the world. It's an exaggeration, but using cryptocurrency is akin to getting access to an almost limitless amount of offshore bank accounts.

For governments accustomed to using financial control (or outright bullying) to keep troublesome elites in line, decentralization poses a challenge. CoinTelegraph published in late 2017 on a global cryptocurrency project led by the Russian government. If successful, the project would have two positive outcomes for those involved: it would weaken the dollar's supremacy as the world's de facto means of trade. It would give participating governments tighter control over the world's growing supply of valuable cryptocurrency.

In most cases, less expensive than traditional electronic transactions Blockchains, private keys, and wallets effectively address the double-spending problem, preventing new cryptocurrencies from being exploited by tech-savvy criminals capable of duplicating digital funds. Cryptocurrencies' security features also remove the need for a third-party payment processor to authenticate and validate any electronic financial transaction, such as Visa or PayPal.

As a result, there is no need for mandatory transaction fees to help the work of payment processors since miners, the cryptocurrency equivalent of payment processors, receive new currency units in addition to discretionary transaction fees for their work. Compared to 1.5 percent to 3 percent for credit card payment processors and PayPal, cryptocurrency transaction fees are usually less than 1% of the transaction amount.

Fewer Barriers and Costs to International Transactions

International transactions are not treated any differently in cryptocurrency than domestic transactions. No matter where the sender and receiver are based, transactions are either free or with a small transaction fee. This is a significant advantage over international transactions involving fiat currency, which almost always include fees that do not apply to domestic transactions, such as international credit cards or ATM fees. Direct foreign money transfers can often be very costly, with fees often reaching 10% or 15% of the transferred volume.

You Will Also Enjoy: Many common credit cards have international transaction fees, which can greatly increase the cost of transactions in other countries.

CONS OF CRYPTOCURRENCY

Lack of Regulation Facilitates Black Market Activity

The potential of cryptocurrency to promote illegal activity is probably its greatest flaw and regulatory concern. Bitcoin and other cryptocurrencies are used in many gray and black market online transactions. Before it was shut down in 2014, Silk Road's notorious dark web platform used Bitcoin to promote illegal drug sales and other unlawful activities. Cryptocurrencies are now becoming more widely used for money laundering, which involves passing illegally acquired funds through a "clean" intermediary to hide their origins.

The same characteristics that make cryptocurrencies difficult for governments to seize and monitor make it relatively easy for criminals to operate – though it should be noted that the maker of Silk Road is now in prison as a result of a years-long DEA investigation.

Tax Evasion Possibility in Some Jurisdictions

Cryptocurrencies are naturally attractive to tax evaders because they are not controlled by national governments and exist outside of their direct control. Many small businesses pay their employees in bitcoin and other cryptocurrencies to avoid paying payroll taxes and help their employees avoid paying income taxes. In contrast, online retailers often accept cryptocurrencies to avoid paying sales and income taxes.

According to the IRS, all cryptocurrency transfers made by and to U.S. individuals and companies are subject to the same taxation guidelines. Many nations, however, do not have such policies in place. Because of the inherent anonymity of cryptocurrency, some tax law violations are difficult to monitor, particularly those involving pseudonymous online sellers (instead of an employer who puts an employee's real name on a W-2 indicating their bitcoin earnings for the tax year).

The Risk of Financial Loss as a Result of Data Loss

Early cryptocurrency supporters claimed that, if properly protected, alternative digital currencies could support a significant shift away from physical cash, which they saw as flawed and potentially dangerous. It's better to store money in the cloud or even a physical data storage unit than in a back pocket or purse, assuming practically unbreakable source code, impenetrable authentication protocols (keys), and sufficient hacking protections.

This, however, assumes that cryptocurrency users take the necessary precautions to prevent data loss. When a user's private keys are stored on a single physical storage unit, for example, the device is lost or stolen, the user suffers permanent financial damage. And users who store their data on a single cloud service risk losing it if the server is physically destroyed or becomes disconnected from the

Internet (a possibility for servers located in countries with tight Internet controls, such as China).

High Price Volatility and Manipulation Potential
Many cryptocurrencies have a small number of outstanding units concentrated in possession of a small number of people (often the currencies' developers and near associates). Like thinly traded penny stocks, these holders essentially regulate the supply of these currencies, rendering them vulnerable to wild price fluctuations and outright exploitation. However, commonly exchanged cryptocurrencies are subject to market fluctuations: In 2017, Bitcoin's value doubled several times before halving in the first few weeks of 2018.

Always unable to be exchanged for fiat money
Only the most common cryptocurrencies – those with the highest market capitalization in dollars – have dedicated online exchanges that allow for direct fiat currency exchange. The rest don't have dedicated online markets, so they can't be traded for fiat currencies directly. Instead, users must convert them into more widely used cryptocurrencies, such as Bitcoin, before converting them to fiat currency. By raising the cost of exchange transactions, demand for and thus the value of certain lesser-used cryptocurrencies is suppressed.

Chargebacks and refunds are limited or non-existent.
Although cryptocurrency miners operate as quasi-intermediaries for cryptocurrency transactions, they cannot resolve conflicts between the parties involved. In reality, a decentralized arbitrator's idea runs counter to the decentralizing impulse at the core of modern cryptocurrency philosophy. This means you have no one to turn to if you're duped in a cryptocurrency deal, such as paying in advance for something you never get. While some newer cryptocurrencies try to solve the chargeback/refund issue, solutions are still in the early stages and are largely unproven.
Traditional payment providers and credit card networks, including Visa, MasterCard, and PayPal, on the other hand, often intervene in buyer-seller conflicts. Their refund plans, also known as chargeback policies, are intended to deter seller fraud.

Adverse Environmental Impacts of Cryptocurrency Mining
Cryptocurrency mining consumes a lot of resources. Bitcoin, the world's most famous cryptocurrency, is the main suspect. Bitcoin mining uses more energy than the entire country of Denmark, according to figures cited by Ars Technica – but without the egalitarian Scandinavian state's negligible carbon footprint, as some of the world's largest Bitcoin mines are located in coal-rich countries like China.

Cryptocurrency experts agree that mining poses a significant environmental hazard at current development rates, even if they are swift to dismiss the most alarmist arguments. According to Ars Technica, there are three potential short- to medium-term solutions:
•   Lowering the price of Bitcoin to make mining less profitable, a move that would almost certainly necessitate concerted intervention in what has so far been a free market.
•   Reducing the mining incentive at a faster pace than planned (halving every four years)
•   Changing to a less power-hungry algorithm, which is a contentious prospect among mining companies.
Longer-term, the best way is to fuel cryptocurrency mines with low- or no-carbon energy sources, possibly with incentives to move mines to low-carbon countries such as Costa Rica and the Netherlands.

EXAMPLES OF CRYPTOCURRENCY

Since the launch of Bitcoin, the use of cryptocurrencies has exploded. Although exact active currency numbers fluctuate and individual currency prices are extremely unpredictable, the aggregate market valuation of all active cryptocurrencies is trending upward. Hundreds of cryptocurrencies are actively traded at any given moment.
The following cryptocurrencies have a steady acceptance rate, high user activity, and a reasonably high market capitalization (in most cases, greater than $10 million, while valuations are subject to change):

1. Bitcoin
Bitcoin is the most commonly used cryptocurrency globally, and it is credited with taking the cryptocurrency trend into the mainstream. Its

market cap and individual unit value consistently outnumber the next most common cryptocurrency (by a factor of 10 or more). The supply of Bitcoin is limited to 21 million units.

Bitcoin is becoming more widely accepted as a legal form of payment. Many well-known businesses accept Bitcoin payments. However, most use an exchange to convert Bitcoin to U.S. dollars before obtaining funds.

2. Litecoin

Litecoin, which was launched in 2011, has the same basic structure as Bitcoin. A higher programmed supply cap (84 million units) and a faster target blockchain construction time are two main differences (two-and-a-half minutes). The encryption algorithm is also a little different. By market capitalization, Litecoin is frequently the second or third most common cryptocurrency.

3. Ripple

Ripple, which was launched in 2012, is known for its "consensus ledger" technology, which significantly reduces transaction confirmation and blockchain formation times. There is no set goal time, but the average is every few seconds. Ripple can also be exchanged more quickly than other cryptocurrencies, thanks to an in-house currency exchange that converts Ripple units into U.S. dollars, yen, euros, and other popular currencies.

Critics also pointed out that Ripple's network and code are more vulnerable to advanced hackers and do not provide the same anonymity level as Bitcoin-derived cryptocurrencies.

4. Ethereum

Ethereum, which was launched in 2015, improves on Bitcoin's basic architecture in several ways. Smart contracts, in particular, are used to enforce the completion of a deal, persuade parties not to break their agreements, and provide mechanisms for refunds if one party breaks the agreement. While "smart contracts" are a significant step toward solving the lack of chargebacks and refunds in cryptocurrencies, it remains to be seen if they will be enough to fully solve the problem.

5. Dogecoin

Dogecoin is a Litecoin variant that is distinguished by its instantly identifiable Shiba Inu mascot. It has a much faster blockchain production time (one minute) and a much larger number of coins in circulation – the founders reached their goal of 100 billion units mined by July 2015, and there is a supply limit of 5.2 billion units mined per year after that, with no defined supply limit. As a result, Dogecoin is notable as an experiment in "inflationary cryptocurrency," and analysts keep a close eye on seeing how its long-term value trend compares to other cryptocurrencies.

6. Coinye

Coinye, a now-defunct cryptocurrency, is notable for its strange backstory alone.

Coinye was founded in 2013 under the moniker "Coinye West" and is distinguished by an unmistakable resemblance to hip-hop superstar Kanye West. In early 2014, shortly before Coinye's launch, West's legal team learned of the currency's existence and sent a cease-and-desist letter to its makers.

To prevent legal repercussions, the developers stripped the word "West" from the name, replaced the logo with a "half guy, half-fish hybrid" that resembled West (a jab at a "South Park" episode mocking West's huge ego), and released Coinye as expected. The currency attracted a cult following among cryptocurrency enthusiasts due to the excitement and ironic humor surrounding its publication. Despite this, West's legal team filed a lawsuit, requiring the founders to sell their shares and shut down Coinye's website.

Though Coinye's peer-to-peer network is still active, and it is still theoretically possible to mine the currency, the currency's value has plummeted to the point that it is practically worthless.

Cryptocurrency is a fascinating idea that has the potential to transform global finance for the better. Although cryptocurrency is built on sound, democratic principles, it is still technical and practical work. Nation-states tend to have a near-monopoly on currency production and monetary policy for the foreseeable future.

Meanwhile, cryptocurrency users (and non-users fascinated by the concept's promise) must be constantly aware of the concept's practical limitations. Any suggestions that a specific cryptocurrency provides complete anonymity or protection from legal liability, as well as claims that individual cryptocurrencies are foolproof investment opportunities or inflation hedges, should be treated with caution. Even though gold is frequently hailed as the ultimate inflation shield, it is nevertheless subject to extreme uncertainty – maybe even more so than many first-world fiat currencies.

CHAPTER 3: THE 10 MOST IMPORTANT

CRYPTOCURRENCIES OTHER THAN BITCOIN

Bitcoin has become the de facto norm for cryptocurrencies, inspiring an ever-growing legion of followers and spinoffs. Bitcoin was not only a trendsetter, ushering in a flood of cryptocurrencies based on a decentralized peer-to-peer network; it has also become the de facto standard for cryptocurrencies, inspiring an ever-growing legion of followers and spinoffs.

- A cryptocurrency, broadly defined, is a type of currency on a distributed and decentralized ledger and is represented by tokens or "coins."
- Also, since Bitcoin's launch over a decade ago, the area of cryptocurrencies has grown exponentially, and the next great digital token may be published tomorrow.
- In terms of market capitalization, user base, and success, Bitcoin continues to lead the cryptocurrencies pack.
- Ethereum and other virtual currencies are being used to build decentralized financial structures for those who do not have access to conventional financial products.
- Some altcoins are being supported because they provide newer features than Bitcoin, such as processing more transactions per second or using various consensus algorithms, such as proof-of-stake.

What Are Cryptocurrencies?
Before we dive into any of these Bitcoin alternatives, let's take a step

back and define what we mean by words like cryptocurrency and altcoin. In its broadest sense, a cryptocurrency is a type of virtual or digital money in the form of tokens or "coins." While some cryptocurrencies have entered the physical world through credit cards or other ventures, the vast majority of cryptocurrencies remain completely intangible.

The term "crypto" refers to the complex cryptography that enables the production and processing of digital currencies and their transactions through decentralized systems. A popular commitment to decentralization goes hand in hand with this critical "crypto" aspect of these currencies; cryptocurrencies are usually built as code by teams who build in mechanisms for issuance (often, but not always, through a process called "mining") and other controls.

Cryptocurrencies are almost always intended to be immune to government exploitation and control, though this fundamental feature of the market has come under fire as it has increased in popularity. Altcoins, and in some cases "shitcoins," are currencies modeled after Bitcoin that have often attempted to portray themselves as enhanced or updated variants of Bitcoin. Although some of these currencies may have some unique features that Bitcoin does not, no altcoin has yet to match the level of protection that Bitcoin's networks provide.

Other than Bitcoin, we'll look at some of the most common digital currencies below. But first, a disclaimer: a list like this can never be completely exhaustive. One explanation for this is that, as of January 2021, there are over 4,000 cryptocurrencies in circulation. Although many of these cryptocurrencies have little or no support or trading volume, others have devoted groups of backers and investors.

Aside from that, the world of cryptocurrencies is constantly evolving, and the next big digital coin may be published tomorrow. Although Bitcoin is generally regarded as the first cryptocurrency, analysts use various methods to evaluate tokens other than BTC. Analysts, for example, often place a high value on the ranking of coins in terms of market capitalization compared to one another. This has been taken into account, but there are other explanations why a digital token could be included in the list.

1. Ethereum (ETH)
Ethereum, the first Bitcoin alternative on our list, is a decentralized

software platform that allows Smart Contracts and Decentralized Applications (DApps) to be designed and run without third-party need downtime, theft, control, or intervention. Ethereum's mission is to build a decentralized suite of financial products that everyone in the world, regardless of nationality, race, or religion, can use for free. This feature heightens the consequences for those in certain countries. Those without access to state infrastructure and identification can obtain bank accounts, loans, insurance, and several other financial items.

Ethereum applications are driven by ether, Ethereum's platform-specific cryptographic token. Ether is used as a mode of transportation on the Ethereum blockchain. It is primarily pursued by developers who want to build and run applications on the platform and investors who want to buy other digital currencies with ether. Ether, which was introduced in 2015, is the second-largest digital currency by market capitalization after Bitcoin, though it is still a long way behind the dominant cryptocurrency. Ether's market cap is about 19 percent of Bitcoin's as of January 2021.

Ethereum launched a pre-sale for ether in 2014, which generated a massive response, ushering in the initial coin offering (ICO) era. Ethereum can be used to "codify, decentralize, protect, and exchange just about anything," according to the company. Following the 2016 DAO assault, Ethereum was split into two parts: Ethereum (ETH) and Ethereum Classic (ETHC) (ETC). Ethereum (ETH) had a market cap of $138.3 billion and a per token value of $1,218.59 in January 2021.

Ethereum intends to move from a proof-of-work to a proof-of-stake consensus algorithm in 2021. This change would enable Ethereum's network to use much less energy while also increasing transaction speed. Proof-of-stake helps users to "stake" their ether on the network. This procedure aids in the security of the network as well as the processing of transactions. Those that do so are compensated with ether, which is equivalent to interest on a savings account. This is an alternative to Bitcoin's proof-of-work scheme, which rewards miners for processing transactions with more Bitcoin.

2. Litecoin (LTC)

Litecoin, which debuted in 2011, was one of the first cryptocurrencies to follow in Bitcoin's footsteps and dubbed the "silver to Bitcoin's gold." Charlie Lee, an MIT graduate and former Google engineer designed it. Litecoin is based on an open-source global payment network that is not managed by any central authority and employs the "scrypt" proof of work, decoded using consumer-grade CPUs. While Litecoin is similar to Bitcoin in several respects, it has a faster block generation rate and faster confirmation time for transactions. An increasing number of retailers, in addition to developers, support Litecoin. Litecoin had a market capitalization of $10.1 billion and a per token value of $153.88, making it the world's sixth-largest cryptocurrency in January 2021.

3. Cardano (ADA)

Cardano is an "Ouroboros proof-of-stake" cryptocurrency developed by engineers, mathematicians, and cryptography experts using a research-based methodology. Charles Hoskinson, one of Ethereum's five original founding members, was a co-founder of the project. After some disagreements with Ethereum's direction, he left and later assisted in the creation of Cardano.

Cardano's blockchain was developed through comprehensive testing and peer-reviewed studies by the Cardano team. The project's researchers have published over 90 articles on blockchain technology covering a wide variety of topics. Cardano's research is its foundation.

Cardano appears to stand out among its proof-of-stake peers and other large cryptocurrencies due to this rigorous method. Cardano has also been nicknamed the "Ethereum killer" because of its blockchain's capabilities. Cardano, on the other hand, is still in its infancy. Although it has beaten Ethereum to the consensus paradigm of proof-of-stake, it still has a long way to go into decentralized financial applications.

Cardano aspires to be the world's financial operating system by creating decentralized financial goods in the same way that Ethereum does and offering solutions for chain interoperability, voter fraud, and legal contract tracking other items. Cardano has a market capitalization of $9.8 billion as of January 2021, and one ADA is worth $0.31.

4. Polkadot (DOT)

Polkadot is a one-of-a-kind proof-of-stake cryptocurrency that aims to provide blockchain interoperability. Its protocol connects permissioned and permissionless blockchains and oracles, allowing systems to collaborate under one roof.

Polkadot's central component is its relay chain, which enables network interoperability. It also allows for "parachains," or parallel blockchains with their native tokens for unique use cases.

Rather than building only decentralized applications on Polkadot, developers can build their blockchain while still benefiting from the protection that Polkadot's chain already provides. Developers can build new blockchains with Ethereum, but they must implement their security measures, which may expose new and smaller projects to attack, as the larger a blockchain is, the more secure it is. Polkadot refers to this term as "shared security."

Gavin Wood, another of the Ethereum project's core founders who had conflicting views on the project's future, created Polkadot. Polkadot has a market capitalization of $11.2 billion as of January 2021, and one DOT is worth $12.54.

5. Bitcoin Cash (BCH)

Since it is one of the earliest and most popular hard forks of the original Bitcoin, Bitcoin Cash (BCH) holds a significant position in altcoins' history. A fork occurs in the cryptocurrency environment as a result of disagreements and debates between developers and miners. Because of the decentralized existence of digital currencies, wholesale adjustments to the code underlying the token or coin in question need consensus; this process's mechanism differs by cryptocurrency.

When various sides can't agree, the digital currency is split. The original chain holds to its original code and the new chain starting as a new version of the previous coin, complete with code changes.

As a result of one of these breaks, BCH was born in August of 2017. The debate that led to the development of BCH revolved around scalability; the Bitcoin network has a block size limit of one megabyte (MB). The block size in BCH has been increased from one MB to eight MB, with the expectation that larger blocks will accommodate more transactions and thereby increase transaction speed. Other improvements include the elimination of the Segregated Witness protocol, which affects block space. BCH had a market cap of $8.9 billion and a token value of $513.45 in January 2021.

6. Stellar (XLM)

Stellar is an open blockchain network that connects financial institutions to provide enterprise solutions for large transactions. Huge transactions between banks and investment companies that used to take days, involve various intermediaries, and cost a lot of money can now be completed almost instantly, with no intermediaries and little to no cost to the parties involved.

Despite its positioning as an enterprise blockchain for institutional transactions, Stellar is still an open blockchain that everyone can use. Cross-border transactions in any currency are possible with the device. Lumens are Stellar's native currency (XLM). For users to be able to transact on the network, they must have Lumens.

Jed McCaleb, a founding member of Ripple Labs and the Ripple protocol creator, created Stellar. He subsequently left Ripple and went on to found the Stellar Development Foundation with his co-founders. As of January 2021, Stellar Lumens have a market capitalization of $6.1 billion and are priced at $0.27.

7. Chainlink

Chainlink is a decentralized oracle network that connects smart contracts, such as those on Ethereum, to data outside the platform. Blockchains can't bind to external applications securely. Smart contracts can communicate with outside data using Chainlink's decentralized oracles, allowing them to be executed based on data that Ethereum itself cannot bind to.

A variety of use cases for Chainlink's framework are detailed on the company's blog. One of the many applications mentioned is monitoring water sources for contamination or illegal siphoning in specific cities. Sensors may be installed to monitor corporate use, water tables, and local water levels. This data could be tracked by a Chainlink oracle and fed directly into a smart contract. With the oracle's incoming data, the smart contract may be set up to issue fines; issue flood alerts to towns, or invoice companies using too much of a city's water.

Sergey Nazarov and Steve Ellis collaborated on Chainlink. Chainlink's market capitalization is $8.6 billion as of January 2021, and one LINK is worth $21.53.

8. Binance Coin (BNB)

Binance Coin is a utility cryptocurrency that can be used to pay for trading fees on the Binance Exchange. Those that use the token to pay for the exchange will sell at a reduced rate. Binance Coin's blockchain also serves as the foundation for Binance's decentralized exchange. Changpeng Zhao created the Binance exchange, one of the most widely used exchanges globally in terms of trading volumes.

Binance Coin was first released as an ERC-20 token on the Ethereum blockchain. It was finally given its mainnet. The network uses a proof-of-stake consensus model. Binance has a market capitalization of $6.8 billion as of January 2021, with one BNB worth $44.26.

9. Tether (USDT)

Tether was one of the first and most common of a class of cryptocurrencies known as stablecoins, which tend to minimize uncertainty by pegging their market value to a currency or other external reference point. Tether and other stablecoins aim to smooth out market fluctuations to draw consumers who may otherwise be wary of digital currencies, including big ones like Bitcoin, which have undergone repeated periods of drastic volatility. The price of Tether is directly linked to the price of the US dollar. The framework enables users to make transactions from other crypto currencies to US dollars faster and more conveniently than converting to regular currency.

Tether, which was established in 2014, describes itself as a "blockchain-enabled platform designed to promote the digital use of fiat currencies." This cryptocurrency effectively enables individuals to transact in conventional currencies using a blockchain network and related technology while avoiding the instability and uncertainty associated with digital currencies. Tether was the third-largest cryptocurrency by market capitalization in January 2021, with a total market capitalization of $24.4 billion and a per token value of $1.00.

10. Monero (XMR)

Monero is a secure, anonymous, and untraceable cryptocurrency. This open-source cryptocurrency was first released in April 2014, and it quickly gained popularity among cryptography enthusiasts. The creation of this cryptocurrency is entirely funded by donations and powered by the group. Monero was created with a strong emphasis on decentralization and scalability, and it uses a technique called "ring signatures" to provide total privacy.

With this method, a group of cryptographic signatures emerges, at least one real participant. Still, since they all appear legitimate, the real one cannot be identified. Monero has gained a shady image due to its outstanding security protocols, and it has been connected to illegal operations all over the world. If Monero is a good candidate for anonymous criminal transactions, its privacy is also beneficial to dissidents in authoritarian regimes worldwide. Monero had a market cap of $2.8 billion and a per token value of $158.37 in January 2021.

CHOOSING A CRYPTOCURRENCY TRADING STYLE THAT IS RIGHT FOR YOU

There are many different ways to trade cryptocurrency. Some types are better suited to a person's preferences, tolerances, and objectives than others.

Scalping, Day Trading, Swing Trading, Intraday Trading, Range Trading, Position Trading, and Investing are different trading types.

While there are various ways to classify trading types, I will classify them as scalping, day trading, intra-day trading, range trading, swing trading, position trading, and investing.

Scalping aims to make very quick moves, day trading aims to make profitable trades during the trading day, range trading refers to trading the current range, intraday is just a term I'm using to describe a type of day trading that occurs over days, swing trading is trading from one set level to another (typically over days or weeks), and position trading is trading over a long time.

These types differ, but the general idea is that we're progressing from the quickest trading style, scalping, to the most long-term trading style, investing.

One may pick a style that fits them or mixes and matches styles depending on their asset or objectives. In any case, it's a good idea to adapt your strategies to fit your trading style, as different tactics work best with different time frames (investors are less concerned with smaller time frames, volatility, and technical support/resistance, and will usually keep their main position unleveraged, while scalpers might try to use leverage to front-run support and resistance on a 5-minute chart).

The best way to figure out which styles suit you best is to experiment with them and be honest with yourself about how good you are and how they impact your emotional and rational well-being.

Simply put, if a style is throwing you off and making you feel off-balanced, it isn't the right style for you (and if you are consistently losing, it isn't the right style for you either).

In certain ways, the faster you make decisions and lose a smaller amount of your bankroll, the less risk you'll have for each transaction on paper, but the more hands-on your trading will be. Meanwhile, since you'll be making a lot of transfers, you'll end up introducing more confusion and having to consider slippage and fees more.

Given the above, position trading and investing are the best options for a new or casual trader, as they require less micromanagement and technical expertise. However, in crypto, those trading/investing forms face additional stress... since the market is unpredictable even over long periods.

Meanwhile, any trading strategy that requires you to keep positions overnight can cause you stress since crypto is a global market that operates 24 hours a day, seven days a week. It is not unusual for price corrections to occur while you are sleeping.

Still, for those who aren't sure, role trading or investing combined with dollar-cost averaging is a good place to start.

NOTE: The types on this page may be referred to as cryptocurrency investment styles. That, however, is a completely different topic. Cryptocurrency trading can be done in a variety of ways. To me, investment styles such as dollar-cost averaging, profit averaging, and so on are more appealing (ways to build long-term positions in assets). The point here is to talk about trading forms, which are ways to construct positions with the intention of profiting, rather than ways to build a position in an asset as a long-term investment (although there is an overlap, and investing terms are discussed).

DIFFERENT STYLES OF CRYPTO TRADING

With that out of the way, here are some more comprehensive examples of trading styles (all of which apply to all forms of trading but will be discussed in the sense of crypto):

Scalping

Scalping entails making extremely fast trades. The aim is to maintain a steady profit stream (even if the profits are very small). Profits will be taken easily, and expenses will be cut just as quickly. You could trade every few minutes, or you could just scalp a few places per day. You're looking for favorable trade setups, not just any trade. You should be able to go both long and short (and would thus need to margin trade, even at 1x leverage, so you can short). You can, however, scalp by buying and selling on the spot (buying and selling crypto).

This form can require you to purchase Ether at $700, sell at $705, then purchase at $702 and sell at $710. In such situations, a close stop may be set at $698. You may also have a rule that if the trade goes against you, you must manually scale out of your spot. You will rarely just let your positions run; you must still set profit goals.

This necessitates constant concentration. You can, however, make fast money if you are good at it.

This makes risk management and a lot of luck or talent, but on paper, you can make small gains all the time, and those gains can easily add up.

TIP: Do some research on risk-reward in trading to help you figure out where to set your stops. If you're scalping, you'll probably want to use stops.

Day Trading

Day trading is exactly what it sounds like: it's similar to scalping, except instead of making trades every few minutes, you make them every day.

A day trader could scalp, trade the range, or even take short-term position trades in a single day. They're day traders because they don't keep their positions for more than one trading day.

You still use stop losses to scale in and out of positions, but you're aiming for a little more benefit per transaction than a scalper, and you're more likely to tolerate uncertainty and let some of your positions fly.

NOTE: Scalping is a form of day trading, but I'm describing them separately since they have different connotations.

Range Trading

Cryptocurrencies can continuously establish a trading range. This selection would most likely be a form of consolidation (either accumulation, big players getting more coins for the next leg up, or distribution, selling coins at a high before the big players let the market drop).

A range trader trades the range and sets stops; they don't care whether they're trading the range at its all-time peak or its local bottom because they're simply purchasing the range's bottom with a stop and selling the range's maximum (or scaling out toward the top). Trading makes sense because there is a variety, so there are strong support and resistance. You concentrate on making lucrative and predictable trades in the current range while others trade the breakout or breakdown.

This can be day trading or intraday trading, but the aim is to trade the range rather than buy into an uptrend or sell after a downtrend.

Intraday Trading

This is day trading, but a form of it that allows you to keep positions for more than one day. It's as easy as that. Traders do it all the time, and there's no reason why they can't be good. Since the crypto market never closes, there is no such thing as a trading day (the best we get is daily candle closes). You can automate positions with software, so there's no need to close a short-term position simply because the clock strikes 4 p.m. or whatever.

Swing Trading

Finding support and trading to the next resistance stage, or more broadly, choosing an entry and an aim and keeping the position until your target is met or other exit conditions are met, is the essence of swing trading.

Here, you'll take place (sometimes gradually) at what you think is the local bottom AKA help, then HODL your position to what you think is the local top AKA resistance (generally gradually scaling out of your position to lock in profits). Shorting is the inverse logic; you want to shorten from the top of the forming pattern to the bottom.

Swing trading is a form of trading that takes place over days or weeks. That means you'll be able to take a seat, sleep on it, watch it rise and fall in waves, and so on, all without panicking.

It can make a lot of sense to concentrate on swing trading if you can get a clear sense of TA, for example, if you feel like you can evaluate trends and detect possible support and resistance levels.

Swing trading is all about reaching the bottom of the wave and riding it to the top as cryptocurrency rises and falls in waves (with long positions; it is the opposite with short positions).

The amount of time you spend depends on the chart's timeline and the pattern you're looking at, but in general, a move will take a long time.

Swing traders who successfully use long and short positions to trade do very well by doing very little work. Detecting the pattern, remaining cool, and losing on stops, on the other hand, takes a lot of guts.

NOTE: I believe swing trading is the most accommodating trading style and the easiest to master because higher time frame support and resistance seem to hold better than lower time frame support and resistance. You don't have to respond to trades as quickly. Swing also allows you to catch memorable runs. If you want to trade, start here; if you'd rather invest than trade but still want to benefit, try role trading.

Position Trading

Position trading is similar to a scaled-up form of swing trading or the trading equivalent of investing. You'll try to build/take a long position low or a short position high and then hold it for weeks, months, or even years.

This is the most basic form of trading, but it also necessitates a great deal of discipline. Consider someone who has been long Bitcoin even though it was $5k and short since it was $12k (BTC is now $8.3k). Bitcoin has risen from a low of $20k to a high of $5k, and from there to a high of $11k. Any of those activities may have been witnessed by a disciplined position trader (although they may be scaled out a few of their position or reopened positions, or maybe they exited completely when the trend turned unfavorable after a considerable drawdown from the top).

Position trading is similar to investing in that it is long-term, but it differs in that the end aim is to make a winning longer-term trade based on broad trends.

In crypto, you must persevere through the wild ups and downs, bear and bull markets, good and bad news, and keep your eye on the prize. TIP: Combine position trading with high-frequency trend signals such as 50 and 200 days MA crosses (feel encouraged to use a more nuanced strategy, I just want to give a simple example). On a bearish cross, you could close a place and then reopen it on a bullish cross. This strategy works best with trending properties, which the big cryptos are.

Investing

Investing and selling are not synonymous, in my view. Taking place and hoping to benefit is the essence of trading. Investing is all about owning an asset that serves as a store of value to raise its value over time.

Warren Buffet is a businessman and an investor. Buying stock makes him feel like he's buying a piece of the business. If you own a Fortune 500 company, you don't want to take income as its value rises; instead, you want to see more growth. A low price denotes a low-cost company (this is not something a trader ever thinks about).

Investors are more likely to sell their stake if they don't like the asset's price trajectory than if they don't like its current dollar value.

An investor doesn't always implement a stop loss. Instead, they'll establish a role in the asset and stick with it for as long as the reason they bought it in the first place is still valid.

If you're a true HODLer, you won't need to look at rates or charts unless you're trying to add to your place at a reasonable price.

While investing is not the same as trading, buys and sells must be made at some point, and it is important to recognize that this style would appeal to some people.

NOTE: You can take a full position or ease into either of the above types. Some people would use accumulation bots to purchase very small quantities of the coin all day, others will reach a spot incrementally with a few buys, and still, others will go all-in on a single swing. It doesn't matter which style you choose as long as it fits you and you have a risk management strategy in place.

TIP: Patience is needed for all of the above types. Nothing is more common than seeing a series of losses in a row while day trading or seeing a downtrend immediately after opening a well-researched long position (or uptrend after a short position). What can go wrong usually does. To see if a style is statically working overtime, you must persevere through the failures; you cannot judge a style or apply a style based on a few outcomes in a short period. The aim is to be correct more often than incorrect, not to be correct 100% of the time. It will take time to refine your style, and your strategies will most likely need to be changed depending on the current market and coin you are focusing on.

HOW TO CHOOSE THE APPROPRIATE STYLE FOR YOU

The best style for a person is unique to that individual. I have some general recommendations to make:

• Find a style that works for you and stick with it until you've mastered it, refined it, and become profitable. If your style isn't working, adjust it to the current environment (for example, if we're stuck in a range, take 5% of your holdings and range trade; don't just go from a position trader to a range trader because of what happened this week as a rule of thumb).

• Nothing can destroy your portfolio faster than being an investor at a high or a day trader at a low (because you're effectively buying high and selling low in those situations).

• There is one thing that is worse than that: not managing risk. Each style necessitates a unique approach to risk management (the more trades you make, the smaller the positions and the tighter the stops should be). Different risk management strategies are needed for different types, the goal is to minimize the downside and give the asset enough room to run. Going all-in with 100x leverage on a single play is rarely a good idea, and not setting stops when day trading is rarely a good idea (unless you are at your computer and will exit trades by hand nimbly, thus acting as your stop).

• Bitcoin trading is a high-level sport. When it comes to trading, I'm not sure there is a more challenging pastime. For months on end, most people would fall flat on their faces (if not years). Worse, if you enter crypto during a bull market, you are unlikely to lose money at first, and you would be unprepared for the downturn (and will start falling on your face later into your game).

• Expect pain and try to learn some lessons; if things are going well, you're probably in a bull market and can prepare for some challenges ahead (it never stays easy for long).

• Try to keep your lessons affordable by using risk management and not switching up a trading style that has been working for a few trades (for example, avoid the thing where you suddenly become a day trader at the bottom or an investor at the top; also avoid the thing where you hit a few stops and then don't take the next trade because you are scared; in terms of statistics, avoid the thing where you hit a few stops and then don't take the next trade because you are scared.

IMPORTANT: Avoid taking other people's advice, making trades based on other people's calls, swapping trading types in the middle of a trade, and so on. I firmly believe that you should find and stick to a trading style that works for you. You can also understand the difference between a bear and a bull market to not trade like a bull in a bear market and vice versa. To be honest, I might talk about my trading style and offer advice here, and I have in the past, but this isn't a page about how to trade; it is a page about trading styles. If you want my advice, stick to swing, place, and investing and trade the pattern.

CHAPTER 4: TRADING PSYCHOLOGY

WHAT IS TRADING PSYCHOLOGY?

Trading psychology refers to the feelings and mental states that influence whether a trader succeeds or fails. Various facets of an individual's character and attitudes that affect their trading activities are referred to as trading psychology. When it comes to assessing trading performance, trading psychology can be just as critical as other factors like expertise, experience, and ability.

Two of the most important aspects of trading psychology are discipline and risk-taking. A trader's ability to execute these aspects is crucial to his or her trading strategy. While fear and greed are the most well-known emotions associated with trading psychology, hope and remorse are also important emotions that influence trading behavior.

• Trading psychology refers to an investor's decision-making process's emotional aspect, explaining why certain decisions tend to be more logical than others.

• The power of greed and fear mainly defines Trading psychology.

• Greed appears to be the driving force behind actions that tend to take on too much risk.

• Fear induces actions that tend to minimize risk while generating insufficient returns.

UNDERSTANDING THE PSYCHOLOGY OF TRADING

Trading psychology is linked to a few distinct emotions and behaviors often used as catalysts for stock trading. Most emotional trading is attributed to either greed or fear, according to traditional market characterizations.

Greed can be described as an unhealthy desire for money, which can sometimes cloud reason and judgment. As a result, this definition of greed-driven investing or trading implies that this emotion often leads traders to various actions. Making high-risk trades, purchasing shares of an untested business or technology simply because the price is that quickly, or buying shares without investigating the underlying investment are examples of this.

Additionally, greed can motivate investors to hold lucrative trades for longer than necessary to extract additional profits or take on large speculative positions. Greed is most visible in the final stages of bull markets when speculation is peak and investors abandon caution.

On the other hand, fear induces traders to close positions prematurely or refrain from taking risks because they fear major losses. During bear markets, fear is palpable, and it is a powerful emotion that can trigger traders and investors to behave irrationally in their hurry to exit the market. Fear often transforms into panic, resulting in major stock selloffs as a result of panic selling.

Regret can lead a trader to enter a trade after initially missing out due to the stock's rapid movement. This is a breach of trading discipline, and it often results in direct losses when security prices fall from their peak peaks.

Technical Analysis

For technical analysts who rely on charting techniques to make trade decisions, trading psychology is crucial. Security charting will reveal a wealth of information about a security's movement. Although technical analysis and charting techniques can help identify patterns for buying and selling opportunities, it also necessitates awareness and intuition for market movements derived from an investor's trading psychology.

In technical charting, there are several occasions where a trader must rely not only on the chart's analysis but also on their knowledge of the security they're tracking and their intuition about how wider factors influence the market. Traders who pay close attention to overall security price influences, discipline, and trust have well-balanced trading psychology, leading to profitable results.

THE IMPORTANCE OF TRADING PSYCHOLOGY

Trading effectively in the capital markets necessitates a wide range of abilities. They include analyzing a company's fundamentals and predicting the course of a stock's trend. However, none of these technical abilities nor the trader's mentality are as significant.

Trading psychology is described as the ability to control emotions, think quickly, and exercise discipline.

Fear and greed are the two most important emotions to comprehend and regulate.

Quick Decisions

Traders are always required to think quickly and make swift decisions, darting in and out of stocks on a whim. They'll need a certain level of mental presence to achieve this. They must also have the ability to stick to their trading strategies and understand when to take gains and losses. Emotions obviously cannot be allowed to get in the way.

•   Investor sentiment always steers market performance in opposite directions from the fundamentals.

•   The good investor can harness the two human emotions that drive this sentiment: fear and greed.

•   Recognizing this will help you develop the discipline and objectivity necessary to profit from other people's emotions.

UNDERSTANDING FEAR

When traders receive bad news about a specific stock or the economy in general, they are understandably concerned. They can overreact and feel compelled to liquidate their holdings and sit on their cash, avoiding further risk. They may prevent some losses, but they may also lose out on some profits if they do so.

Fear is a normal reaction to a perceived danger, which traders must recognize. It is a challenge to their profit potential in this situation.

It would be beneficial to quantify the anxiety. Traders should think about what they're afraid of and why they're afraid. The thought, however, should come before the bad news, not after it.

The two visceral feelings to keep in check are fear and greed.

Traders will know how they unconsciously interpret and respond to events if they think about it ahead of time, and they will be able to step beyond the emotional reaction. Of course, this isn't easy, but it's critical to the health of an investor's portfolio, as well as the investor's health.

DEFEATING GREED

On Wall Street, there's an adage that "pigs get slaughtered." This applies to greedy investors' practice of holding on to a winning position for too long to get every last penny out of it. The pattern will eventually reverse, and the greedy will be trapped.

Greed is a difficult foe to defeat. It's usually motivated by a desire to do better, to get a little more. A trader should understand this impulse and establish a trading strategy based on logic rather than whims or instincts.

Creating Guidelines

When the psychological crunch hits, a trader must build rules and stick to them. Establish rules on when to join and exit trades based on your risk-reward tolerance. Set a profit goal and a stop loss to exclude emotion from the equation.

You may also choose which particular events, such as a positive or negative earnings report, can prompt you to buy or sell a stock.

It's a good idea to set daily limits on how much you're willing to win or lose. Take the money and run if you meet the profit mark. If your losses reach a certain threshold, fold your tent and return home.

You'll live to trade another day in either case.

Reviewing and conducting research

Traders must learn what they can about the stocks and sectors that concern them. Keep up with the press, educate yourself, and attend trading seminars and conferences if necessary.

Give the study process as much time as possible. Studying maps, interacting with executives, reading trade papers, and doing other background work such as macroeconomic or market analysis are all examples of this.

Fear may also be overcome with knowledge.

Stay Flexible

Traders must maintain flexibility and consider experimenting from time to time. You may, for example, think about using options to reduce risk. Experimentation is one of the most effective ways for a trader to understand (within reason). The experience could also aid in the reduction of emotional influences.

Finally, traders should evaluate their success regularly. Traders should focus on how they trained for a trading session, how up-to-date they are on the markets, and how they're doing in terms of continuing education, in addition to evaluating their returns and individual positions. This periodic evaluation will help correct trader errors, change bad habits, and improve overall returns.

TRADING'S THREE ENEMIES

For most traders, managing emotions and mastering inner psychology is the most difficult task. It's one thing to have a good plan, but it's another to put it into action without allowing your emotions to sabotage your trades.

Self-awareness and discipline are needed to become a consistent trader. Identifying the inner demons that get in your way is the first step toward enhancing your trades.

1: FEAR

Fear is a trader's greatest enemy; it will do all it can to disrupt your trades and divert you from your strategy. You'll overanalyze the markets and tinker with your trades because you're afraid of losing money.

Fear of failure leads to the following common trading blunders:

- Hesitating when you should act
- Reducing profit margins
- Failure to carry out your strategy
- Panic sale at the bottom of the market
- Obsessing over every blip on the graphs

Solution: Before conducting a deal, determine how much money you're willing to lose. While not every trade will be a winner, your winners will far outnumber your losers if you have a good plan.

Another inner demon that must be confronted is the fear of losing out. It will try to persuade you to follow the hype and invest in an already booming market. If you give in to the urge to chase the markets, you'll almost certainly end up buying a top as the price moves against you.

Solution: Instead of agonizing about a lost opportunity, look for a successful trade in a different market. Accept that you won't be able to capture them all.

2: IMPATIENCE

Patience is a key component of efficient trading. A cat cautiously stalks its prey, waiting for the right moment to strike. You need to be patient and wait for the right opportunity to come along. The best trade is sometimes none at all.

Overtrading the markets almost always results in a loss. In most cases, you have a 50/50 chance of winning, and successful traders look for market inefficiencies that offer them a better chance.

Impatience will cause you to exit a perfectly good trade before seeing it through to its conclusion. It's not uncommon for a swing trade to take months before you see the expected returns.

Solution: Build a trading strategy and follow it through to completion. Determine your entry, exit, stop-loss, and the length of time you're able to keep the trade when creating your strategy. Make it a practice to choose quality over quantity.

3: REGRET

Traders can be hard on themselves if they lose money or miss out on a lucrative opportunity. It's impossible to conduct every single trade flawlessly. It is possible that you won't get the tops and bottoms exactly right. You're still expected to make errors now and then.

Regret will amplify all of your negative fears and make you doubt your trading skills. This can send you down a path of toxic thought, clouding your judgment.

Solution: If you make a mistake, try to learn from it as soon as possible. Recapitulate your skills, find areas for improvement, and then let go. If you're upset and depressed, it's time to take a break before you've calmed down.

HERE IS A LIST OF GOOD TRADING HABITS.

• <u>Rule 1: Recognize the true nature of the markets</u>.
Learn how to make money and what you can do with it. Markets are what are known as disorderly economies. The mathematics of studying such non-linear, dynamic systems is known as chaos theory. Chaotic systems, among other things, may generate results that seem random but are not.

A chaotic economy is inefficient, and forecasting for the long term is difficult. With a trend component, market price movement is highly random.

Commodity traders who have been unsuccessful and disappointed want to assume that the markets are orderly. They believe that prices shift in predictable and well-hidden patterns. They want to believe that they will learn the "key" to the pricing mechanism and gain an advantage.

They believe that highly efficient methods of forecasting future price direction can lead to profitable trading. Since the markets began trading, they have been falling for bogus methods and schemes.

The reality is that, even in the broadest sense, markets are unpredictable.

Fortunately, good trading does not necessitate the use of accurate prediction mechanisms.

Following trends in whatever period you want is important for successful trading. Your competitive advantage is based on the current trend. You can make money in the long run if you observe patterns and use correct money management strategies and business selection.

Good market selection refers to picking good trending markets in general rather than picking a specific circumstance that is likely to produce an immediate pattern.

For traders, two issues are intertwined. The first is to use a good approach that is consistent enough to give you a statistical advantage. The second step is to stick with the method long enough for the edge to appear.

• <u>Rule 2: Take control of your trading destiny.</u>
Examine your trading habits. Recognize your motives. Traders enter the market with the intention of profiting. They find the trading

process interesting, exciting, and critically challenging after a while. The desire to have fun and fulfill the challenge quickly takes precedence over the desire to make money.

The more you trade for the sake of entertainment and ego massage, the more likely you are to lose. The types of trading behaviors that are most amusing are also the ones that are the least reliable. The more you can put a premium on making money over having fun, the more likely you will succeed.

Be mindful of putting your future in the hands of others. The majority of the people you trust are unlikely to be effective traders. Brokers, gurus, consultants, device suppliers, and colleagues, for example. There are a few exceptions, but they are few.

Only depend on others for clerical assistance or to assist you in making decisions. Don't hold anyone responsible for your mistakes.

It's all too easy to fall into this trap. You put yourself in the situation regardless of what happens. As a result, you are ultimately responsible for the outcome. You won't be able to change your bad habits until you accept responsibility for everything.

• <u>Rule 3: Only trade with tried and true methods.</u>

Before you trade, test it out. Most trading methods do not work when used consistently. Most of the conventional wisdom found in books is ineffective.

It's worth noting that authors never show how effective their methods are. The best you can hope for is a few well-chosen examples.

This is because they are lazy, and their strategies are often ineffective when rigorously checked.

Make a strong first impression.

Follow these five trading cardinal rules:
1.   Trade in the direction of the trend.
2.   Minimize the losses.
3.   Let the money roll in.
4.   Balance and diversify your positions.
5.   Minimize risk and keep costs under control.

These are common cliches. Despite this, nearly every losing trader regularly breaks these rules.

Buying power and selling weakness is what trading with the pattern entails. The nature of top and bottom picking is that most traders are more comfortable buying weakness and selling power.

Invest in liquid markets. Your only competitive advantage is to be on the cutting edge of fashion. You should focus on the markets that are trending the most. Over time, this will increase the statistical advantage.

• Rule 4: Trade in proportion to your resources.

Keep your desires in check. Don't put too much money into your account. A representation of greed is one of the most pernicious roadblocks to success. Commodity trading is appealing because it allows you to make a lot of money in a short amount of time.

Surprisingly, the more you strive to meet that expectation, the less likely you are to succeed.

The industry's widespread hype leads people to believe that they will produce impressive results if they work hard enough. Danger, on the other hand, is often proportional to reward. The higher the return you get, the greater the risk you will have to take.

Even if you use a strategy that gives you a statistical advantage, which almost no one does, you will always have to endure excruciating drawdowns on the path to eventual success.

Your drawdowns would be higher the larger the return you attempt. A reasonable rule of thumb is to anticipate an equity drawdown of about 40% of your expected annual benefit. As a result, if you aim for annual returns of 100%, you can expect to lose 40% of your investment. Even the most bullish traders would normally accept a maximum drawdown of this size. Almost no one can sustain their trading system by 50% drawdowns.

It's best to aim for lower returns first before you get the hang of sticking to your system despite the ups and downs that everyone goes through.

According to an experienced money management executive, skilled money managers should be happy with consistent annual returns of 20%. What can you be pleased with if talented professionals are satisfied with that?

I assume that annual returns in the 30-50 percent range are achievable for a good mechanical system diversified in good markets. This type of trading will also result in drawdowns of up to 25% of equity on occasion.

• Rule 5. Manage risk.

When creating your trading strategy or scheme, keep the possibility of failure in mind. When choosing a place to sell, keep the possibility of trading in mind. Manage the possibility of unanticipated occurrences. Manage the danger of each exchange separately.

The chance of disaster is a mathematical term that describes the likelihood of losing something if you have a poor string of luck. If you flip a coin 1,024 times, you can at least once get ten heads in a row. As a result, if you lose 10% of your account on each exchange, you will most likely be wiped out before long.

If you lose 10% of your capital per transaction and your trading method is 55% accurate (and who is?), you still have a 12% chance of being wiped out before doubling your capital.

This means that you win or lose the same amount on each exchange for the mathematicians out there. That is impractical, but I'm merely attempting to explain the problem of ruin danger. The argument is that you must control the amount you risk on each trade to minimize the harm caused by inevitable strings of losses.

The market you trade is another source of risk. Some markets are riskier and more volatile than others. Some markets are quieter than others. Some markets, such as currencies, are more prone to overnight gaps, which raise risks. Lower liquidity and worse fills in some markets add to the risk.

Prioritize risk management over maximizing income.

The most important aspect of risk management is to keep each trade's risk low. Stops should always be included. Always have an eye on the economy. When it comes to minimizing losses, never give in to fear or hope. One of the simplest things a trader can do to improve his long-term success is to avoid major individual losses.

• Rule 6: Maintain a long-term perspective.

Don't make changes to your strategy based solely on short-term results. Instant gratification is emphasized in our culture. We're depleting our long-term assets.

This would eventually result in a drop in our standard of living compared to what it might have been to pay more attention to the future.

Most traders put so much of their pride into their trading that they can't take losses. A string of defeats can be devastating. As a result, they test trading strategies and processes based on extremely short-term performance.

According to statisticians, a measurement has no statistical reliability because there are 30 events to calculate. In the absence of a sufficient number of events, the result is entirely dependent on chance. Strings of losses are as certain as government inefficiency, as we saw in the chance of ruin discussion above.

As a result, a trader who abandons his scheme after four losses in a row is doomed to spend the rest of his trading career switching systems. Do not start trading a system based on a few trades, and do not lose faith in a system based on a few losses. Examine your success over several trades and over some time.

• Rule 7: Maintain a proper perspective while trading.

If you're doing well or not, trading is an emotionally draining experience. It's all too tempting to get caught up in the moment's emotions and make strategic and tactical errors.

When you're having a good time, don't get too excited. One of the most common blunders made by traders is to increase their trading after a, particularly profitable time.

This is the worst thing you can do because good times still come after bad ones. If you boost your trading just before the bad times, you'll lose twice as much money as you make. The most difficult issue for effective traders is figuring out how to maximize trading in a growing account.

When it comes to expanding your trading, be careful. After losses or equity drawdowns are the best opportunities to incorporate. During drawdowns, try not to get too depressed. Trading is similar to golf. Golfers, regardless of talent, go through phases of good and bad play. When a golfer is doing well, he believes he has discovered a trick to his swing and will never perform poorly. He thinks he'll never get out of his slump because he's hitting it sideways.

Trading is a lot like that. When you're making profits, you're thinking about how great trading is and how you can extend your trading to gain enormous wealth. When you're losing money, it's natural to consider quitting trading altogether.

You can handle all emotional extremes with a little practice. You'll probably never be able to fully control them, but don't let your emotions drive you to make unwise adjustments in your approach.

Don't depend on trading as your primary source of stimulation in life because it's dull. Unfortunately, the appealing features of trading, such as simple analysis and trade range, work against you. Trading is monotonous and repetitive. As a result, if you depend on trading for your main source of excitement, pursuing fun will almost certainly result in a loss. Good if you can afford it. If not, look for something else to do with your time.

CHAPTER 5: THE BEST CRYPTOCURRENCY EXCHANGES

Investing in Bitcoin or other cryptocurrencies, or trading them, can be daunting at first. Scams and people losing money are often reported in the news. Although this is real, and many scams have occurred and continue to occur, investing in and safely trading in cryptocurrency has never been easier than today.

When it comes to exchanging and buying Bitcoin and other cryptocurrencies, the most important consideration is safety and protection. The following exchanges are the best for any use case you might have if you wish to buy and keep for a long time, trade regularly, want anonymity or privacy, or simply want the ease of use.

This list includes the best exchanges for different types of traders and the best exchanges within each category. Investing in Bitcoin or other cryptocurrencies can be done in a variety of ways. Please continue reading after the list of exchanges to learn more about how the exchange styles vary. It's important to practice safe storage after you've agreed on an exchange.

2021's Top Crypto Exchanges

- Coinbase and Coinbase Pro are the best overall.
- Cash App is the best for beginners.
- Binance is the best exchange for altcoins.
- Bisq is the best-decentralized exchange.

IN GENERAL, THE BEST

COINBASE

Coinbase and Coinbase Pro are two different types of cryptocurrency exchanges

Fees range from $0.99 to $2.99, depending on the dollar amount spent.

Coinbase is the most well-known and commonly used cryptocurrency exchange in the United States. Coinbase is a fully regulated and licensed cryptocurrency exchange established in 2012, not long after the code for Bitcoin was released in 2009. Coinbase currently has operating licenses in over 40 states and territories in the United States.

Advantages
- A wide range of altcoins to choose from
- Extremely user-friendly app
- Extremely high liquidity

Disadvantages
- Exorbitant fees if you don't use Coinbase Pro
- The user has no power over the wallet keys.
- Trading options for altcoins are limited compared to other exchanges.

Coinbase has largely prevented controversy in the cryptocurrency business, which counterfeit coins and shady exchanges have plagued. Coinbase provides an incredibly user-friendly exchange, lowering the barrier to entry for cryptocurrency investment, which is otherwise perceived as complex and confusing.

Investors and traders can also store their funds in Coinbase's insured custodial wallets. It's important to remember that if your account is hacked due to your actions, this insurance will not cover you. These custodial accounts are ideal for younger users just having their feet wet, but Coinbase owns the private keys to the coins contained inside them, not the investor.

Coinbase also provides the free Coinbase Pro edition, which has a distinct but less expensive fee structure and slightly more charting and indicator options. Coinbase Pro is a great next move for those who've had their feet wet with Coinbase. It helps fill out the overall offering by incorporating functionality that a more experienced consumer might appreciate.

CASH APP

Fees: For each transaction, Cash App charges a service fee. It also assesses a premium based on market fluctuations. These fees fluctuate based on market behavior.

Cash App, like Venmo, is a peer-to-peer money transfer service. Users may use this form of service to split food, pay rent to a roommate, or even shop online at a store that accepts cash. Cash App can act as a bank account, with users having their own Cash App debit cards. This service is easy enough on its own, but Cash App adds even more functionality.

Advantages
• Venmo or Zelle, a peer-to-peer money transfer service
• Bitcoin withdrawal capability
• Extremely user-friendly app

Disadvantages
• At this point, only Bitcoin can be invested in; no other cryptocurrencies are permitted.
• A 3% fee applies when sending money using a connected credit card.
• A maximum of $2,000 in Bitcoin can be withdrawn every 24 hours and $5,000 every seven days.

Similar to Robinhood, Cash App helps its users invest in stocks, ETFs, and cryptocurrency. This exchange's mobile-first interface is simple to understand and use, making it suitable for first-time investors.

Although it has a payment mechanism similar to Venmo and an investment platform similar to Robinhood, Cash App is unique. It enables users to withdraw cryptocurrency investments to their wallets. This is one of the key reasons we choose Cash App over Robinhood as the best Bitcoin wallet for beginners.

In the cryptocurrency culture, the ability to remove cryptocurrency from an exchange is important. You can invest and swap cryptocurrency with Robinhood, but you can't withdraw or spend it. This idea is known in the crypto community as "not your keys, not your coin." This ensures that if you do not hold the private keys to the wallet the coins are held in, they are technically not owned by you.

BINANCE IS THE BEST FOR ALTCOINS

Fees: On the taker side, 0.1 percent, and on the manufacturer side, 0.1 percent. This drops to 0.02 percent on both sides of the exchange as trade volume increases. Fees are reduced by 25% when using Binance's native cryptocurrency, BNB.

Binance is a cryptocurrency exchange that was founded in 2017 with a strong emphasis on altcoin trading. Binance has over 100 different trading pairs available between various cryptocurrencies. There are some fiat-crypto pairs available, but the majority of its pairs are between cryptocurrencies.

Advantages

•   Fees are lower than those charged by other widely used exchanges.

•   A large number of cryptocurrencies and trading pairs to choose from

•   Charting that is more mature

Disadvantages

•   Intended for more experienced users

•   Binance is a cryptocurrency exchange. While the United States has fewer trading pairs than its foreign equivalent, it still has over 100.

•   Binance US does not help 22 US states, including New York.

Binance currently dominates the global exchange market, accounting for a large portion of the regular crypto trading volume. The exchange only accepts U.S. Dollar deposits via SWIFT from international users. Still, it does allow you to buy a limited range of cryptocurrencies directly with a credit or debit card. Deposits in 12 other fiat currencies, including the Euro, are permitted.

Binance is best for those interested in trading or investing in lesser-known altcoins. Binance provides more than 50 different cryptocurrencies to sell, while Coinbase comes in second with 46. While it can seem to be a minor distinction, each coin provides users with more options. Binance is the best exchange for someone interested in trading altcoins or needs more sophisticated charting than most other exchanges offer.

Trading commissions are paid in BTC or BSQ (the network's native cryptocurrency). The cost of trading one Bitcoin is 0.10 percent on the maker side and 0.70 percent on the taker side when fees are paid in Bitcoin. The fees for trading one Bitcoin in BSQ are 0.05 percent on the maker side and 0.35 percent on the taker side.

The fundamental principle of Bitcoin is that it provides transparent and unrestricted access to a unit of account. For instance, banking services, such as a checking or savings account, are only available if you have legally verifiable government identification. This isn't possible for Bitcoin. It is accessible to everyone, regardless of nationality or position, and no identification is needed.

Advantages
*   Non-KYC, decentralized network
*   There are 30 different payment options available, like Zelle.
*   Apps for both Android and iOS devices

Disadvantages
*   Depending on the payment method, transaction speed can be sluggish.
*   Trading rates can be insignificant.
*   This product is not intended for direct trading.

Although some argue that this accessibility allows for illegal activity (the same could be said of using cash), it also provides individuals in countries with less developed financial structures with direct access to units of account. Millions of citizens worldwide lack access to bank accounts or trade because their countries lack the required financial infrastructure or because they lack government-issued identification. In these situations, Bitcoin combined with a decentralized exchange like Bisq can be a good solution.

Bisq is a peer-to-peer decentralized Bitcoin and cryptocurrency exchange that can be downloaded. This means that, like Bitcoin, Bisq has no single point of failure and cannot be taken down. Bisq is non-custodial, which means that no one except the recipient has access to or influence over the funds. This differs from centralized exchanges such as Coinbase, which holds the user's funds in a custodial account over which the user has no access. If Coinbase believes your account activity is suspicious, it has the right to seize your funds, whether or not the activity is illegal in your area.

Since there is no registration process or KYC (Know Your Customer) law, Bisq is immediately open to anyone with a smartphone device. This makes it suitable for those seeking anonymity, activists living under authoritarian regimes, or those without government-issued identification.

Bisq provides trading of many different fiat currencies like USD and Bitcoin and a host of other cryptocurrencies. Its decentralized and peer-to-peer characteristics can mean low trading volumes and slower transactions, but this is well worth it for others.

UNDERSTANDING THE TYPES OF CRYPTO EXCHANGES

To choose the best exchange for your needs, it is important to thoroughly understand the types of exchanges.

Centralized Exchange

The centralized exchange is the first and most popular form of exchange. Coinbase, Binance, Kraken, and Gemini are examples of famous exchanges in this group. These are private companies that have cryptocurrency trading platforms. The Know Your Customer, or Know Your Client; the rule requires registration and identification for these transactions.

All of the above markets have active trading, high volumes, and liquidity. Centralized exchanges, on the other hand, are incompatible with the Bitcoin theory. They run on their private servers, creating an attack vector. If the company's computers are hacked, the whole system may be shut down for some time. Worse, proprietary information about its users can be made public.

The larger, more well-known centralized exchanges provide by far the easiest on-ramp for new users, and they also provide some kind of protection if their systems malfunction. Although this is valid, when you buy cryptocurrency on these exchanges, it is deposited in their custodial wallets rather than your wallet, which you control. The issued protection is only available if the exchange is at fault. Your funds would be lost if your machine and Coinbase account were both compromised, and you would be unable to claim protection. This is why it is important to remove large amounts of money and store them safely.

Decentralized Exchange

Decentralized exchanges work in the same way as Bitcoin. There is no central point of control in a decentralized exchange. Instead, think of it as a server, except that each computer within it is distributed worldwide, and a single person manages each computer that makes up one portion of the server. If one of these computers fails, the network as a whole is unaffected since there are plenty of other computers to keep the network going.

This is in direct contrast to a single company controlling a single server in a single location. Attacking anything that is dispersed and decentralized in this way is far more complicated, making such attacks implausible and likely futile.

Because of this decentralization, these forms of exchanges are not subject to any regulatory agency's rules since a single individual or party does not control the mechanism. Individuals who participate come and go, so a government or regulatory body can't reasonably target any one person or community. This ensures that those who trade on the platform are not required to reveal their identities and are free to use the platform in whatever way they see fit, whether legal or illegal.

CHAPTER 6: FUNDAMENTAL ANALYSIS

Fundamental research looks at a company's internal and external, qualitative and quantitative variables, typically the company bringing a stock or bond issue to market or the "issuer." Analysts look at everything from market trends and the environment to microeconomic variables like the effectiveness of a management team when determining the importance of defense. Fundamental analysis seeks to determine an asset's "right" or "intrinsic" value rather than forecasting future price movements. Fundamental analysis assumes that the market will price security incorrectly in the short term but that the market will ultimately correct itself to represent the security's true value.

If you've calculated a security's intrinsic value, you can use it as a benchmark to see if it's overvalued, undervalued, or priced reasonably. Knowing whether to purchase, sell, or keep an asset requires an understanding of its intrinsic value. For instance, you could benefit by purchasing an asset when it is "incorrectly" undervalued by the market and then selling it once it has reached fair value.

CRYPTOCURRENCY FUNDAMENTAL ANALYSIS

Fundamental analysis can be applied to almost any asset due to its emphasis on intrinsic value, which is important in investment decisions. The fundamental analysis covers a wide variety of disciplines, methods, and principles, but not all are suitable for every asset. It all comes down to deciding which resources to use with which asset classes and why. Suppose you're an equity analyst, for example. In that case, you could look at a company's balance sheet, share price, earnings per share (EPS), and price-to-earnings (P/E) ratio, as well as a variety of other metrics and variables. If you're a foreign exchange (forex) trader, on the other hand, you'll consider completely different variables, such as central bank data that helps decide the state of a country's economy.

However, since a company does not provide cryptocurrencies, how can fundamental analysis determine a crypto asset's underlying value? You will examine the surrounding factors that might affect the asset, just as you would any other asset. To name a few possible indicators, you might assess the cryptocurrency industry's condition, the business as a whole, the domestic and global economic climate, supply and demand, and the competitive landscape.

Other fundamentals that could relate to cryptocurrencies include:

• Whitepaper: In bitcoin, a whitepaper is the equivalent of a company's prospectus. According to the Securities and Exchange Commission, a company offering new security will first issue a preliminary prospectus, then a final prospectus (SEC). The prospectus provides all of the details you'll need to make an informed decision about whether or not to invest in the safe. Similarly, in the crypto world, a whitepaper gives you all the information you need to know about the asset's expected use case, requirements, and goals.

Since crypto whitepapers aren't yet created in collaboration with a regulatory body, it's a good idea to double-check any claims that seem too wide.

• Team (Project Creators): Is there a particular team behind this cryptocurrency? If so, what is the track record of its members? How long have they been working with cryptocurrencies? What other initiatives have they undertaken? What are the histories and skillsets of the team members? If there isn't a team or website behind the asset, you might look into the developer community or, if the project has one, the public GitHub.

• The Crypto Asset's Target Market: Who is the crypto asset aimed at? What is the size of the target market, if we know? What is the asset's purpose or use case? Is it attempting to replace a legacy system? Or do you want to fill a specific void?

• Developers: It's a good idea to look at the number of contributors and activity around a particular asset. Since some cryptocurrencies are still in the early stages of growth, the number of developers working on a project may be a good indicator of its success. It's also a sign of the executive team's dedication to achieving their goals. GitHub shows that Bitcoin has the most developers working on its code, followed by Ethereum. For new investors, a project with few developers should be treated with caution.

• A Word on Rumors: Informal conversations or things you overhear aren't always reliable sources of information while doing research. Knowing what respected colleagues think about a team or a project, particularly if there are any possible red flags, can be extremely beneficial. What is the consensus on this new initiative? Does the project seem to others to be feasible? What does it have to do with the rest of what's going on in the industry? Look online if you don't usually "hear" this information. The grapevine, such as it is, can be found in chat apps or on message boards like Reddit and Bitcointalk. When doing your research, be wary of taking rumors into account.

A Work in Progress

Security Analysis was first published in 1934, but it wasn't the only year in which it was published. Following the stock market crash and Great Depression of 1929, the SEC opened its doors in 1934 to regain public trust. The public viewed securities as highly risky due to these events; the public was wary of financial markets, and the SEC's first order was to control the US securities industry. The Securities and Exchange Commission (SEC) demanded detailed reports from all market participants so that investors could get basic financial information and appreciate the risks of investing in securities. As a result, there is a wealth of information available about publicly traded stocks, financial strategies, laws and regulations, and so on.

However, this is not the case for cryptography. The sector is still very young, with just 11 years under its belt. Remember that the first stock was publicly traded on the New York Stock Exchange (NYSE) in 1817, 117 years before the United States markets were controlled. Furthermore, it appears that there is a rising consensus that cryptocurrency technology, networks, and cryptocurrency assets have intrinsic value. The proper definition and quantification of that value is a work in progress that can be aided by using some applicable fundamental analysis concepts and techniques.

CHAPTER 7: INITIAL COIN OFFERING

What Is an Initial Coin Offering (ICO) and How Does It Work?

The cryptocurrency industry's equivalent of an initial public offering (IPO) is an initial coin offering (ICO) (IPO). An ICO is a method of raising funds for a business seeking to produce a new coin, app, or service.

Interested investors will purchase a new cryptocurrency token provided by the company in exchange for their investment. This token may be useful in utilizing its product or service or simply reflecting a stake in the company or project.

Initial Coin Offerings (ICOs) is a common funding tool for startups who want to sell products and services in the cryptocurrency and blockchain room.

Initial coin offerings (ICOs) are similar to bonds, but they can also be used to fund a software service or product.

Some initial coin offerings (ICOs) have resulted in huge profits for investors. Many others have been exposed as frauds, have failed, or have performed poorly.

To participate in an ICO, you'll need to first buy a digital currency and have a clear understanding of how to use cryptocurrency wallets and exchanges.

Since ICOs are largely unregulated, investors must proceed with extreme caution and vigilance when researching and investing in them.

WHAT IS AN INITIAL COIN OFFERING (ICO), AND HOW DOES IT WORK?

When a cryptocurrency company seeks to raise capital through an initial coin offering (ICO), it normally produces a whitepaper that explains what the project is about, the need the project would serve until it is completed, how much money is required, how much virtual tokens the founders will hold, what form of money would be accepted, and how long the ICO campaign will last.

During the ICO campaign, project backers and enthusiasts purchase some of the project's tokens using fiat or digital currency. The buyers refer to these coins as tokens, and they are equivalent to shares of a company offered to investors during an initial public offering (IPO).

If the funds raised fall short of the firm's minimum requirements, the money could be returned to the backers; at this stage, the ICO is considered a failure. The money raised is used to fulfill the project's objectives if the funding criteria are met within the prescribed timeline.

While initial coin offerings (ICOs) are not controlled, the Securities and Exchange Commission (SEC) has the authority to intervene. The maker of Telegram, for example, raised $1.7 billion in an ICO in 2018 and 2019. Still, the SEC filed an emergency lawsuit. It secured a temporary restraining order due to suspected criminal activity by the production team. 1 The United States District Court for the Southern District of New York granted a preliminary injunction in March 2020, requiring Telegram to refund $1.2 billion to investors and pay an $18.5 million civil penalty.

SPECIAL CONSIDERATIONS

Investors interested in investing in initial coin offerings (ICOs) should first become acquainted with the cryptocurrency space in general. Most ICOs require investors to purchase tokens using pre-existing cryptocurrencies. This means that an ICO investor would need a cryptocurrency wallet for a currency like bitcoin or ethereum and a wallet capable of keeping the token or currency they want to buy.

How does one go about looking for ICOs to invest in? There is no easy way to keep up with the new ICOs. Reading up on new ventures online is the best thing an interested investor can do. ICOs create many buzzes, and there are many places online where investors meet to talk about potential opportunities. There are dedicated sites that aggregate ICOs, enabling investors to learn about new offers and compare them to one another.

ICO (Initial Coin Offering) vs. IPO (Initial Public Offering): What's the Difference? (IPO)

Traditional businesses have a few options for raising the funds they need for growth and expansion. A business can start small and expand as its revenues allow, with only the company owners as its creditors. This, however, implies that they will have to wait a long time for funds to accumulate. Companies may also seek early funding from outside investors, who will provide them with a fast infusion of cash in exchange for a portion of their ownership interest. Another choice is to go public and raise funds from private investors by selling shares in an initial public offering (IPO).

While IPOs only deal with investors, ICOs, including crowdfunding events, can deal with supporters who want to invest in a new project. However, ICOs vary from crowdfunding in that ICO supporters are driven by the potential for a return on their investment, while crowdfunding projects are essentially donations. ICOs are referred to as "crowdsales" for these reasons.

At least two structural variations exist between ICOs and IPOs. First, ICOs are completely unregulated, which means they are not supervised by government agencies such as the Securities and Exchange Commission (SEC). 3 Second, ICOs are far more structure-free than IPOs due to their decentralization and lack of control.

ICOs can be arranged in several different ways. In certain cases, a company will set a particular funding target or cap, which ensures that each token sold in the ICO will have a pre-determined price, and the total token supply will remain constant. In other situations, there is a fixed supply of ICO tokens but a variable funding target, which means that the allocation of tokens to investors is contingent on the amount of money raised (i.e., the more total funds received in the ICO, the higher the overall token price).

On the other hand, others have a dynamic token supply determined by the amount of funding collected. A token price is fixed in these situations, but the total number of tokens is unlimited (save for ICO length parameters).

INITIAL COIN OFFERINGS: BENEFITS AND DRAWBACKS (ICO)

In an initial public offering (IPO), an investor receives shares of a company's stock in return for her money. There are no shares per se in the case of an ICO. Instead, businesses raising funds via an ICO issue a cryptocurrency token, which is the blockchain equivalent of a share. In most cases, investors swap an existing common token—such as bitcoin or ethereum—for an equal number of new tokens.

It's worth noting how simple it is for a business to build tokens through an ICO. Online services make it possible to generate cryptocurrency tokens in a matter of seconds. When comparing the differences between shares and tokens, investors should bear in mind that a token has no intrinsic value or legal guarantees. ICO managers create tokens by the ICO terms, collect them, and then allocate them to individual investors according to their schedule.

Early investors in an ICO are typically enticed to purchase tokens hoping that the venture will succeed once launched. If this occurs, the value of the tokens they bought during the ICO will rise above the ICO price, resulting in net profits. The opportunity for extremely high returns is the primary advantage of an ICO.

Many investors have become millionaires as a result of ICOs. In 2017, for example, 435 initial coin offerings (ICOs) were successful, with each raising an average of $12.7 million. As a result, the overall amount generated in 2017 was $5.6 billion, with the top ten projects accounting for 25% of the total. Furthermore, in dollar terms, tokens purchased in ICOs returned an average of 12.8 times the initial investment. 4

With the rise of ICOs in the cryptocurrency and blockchain industries, they've brought with them new challenges, threats, and opportunities. Many people invest in ICOs in the hopes of getting a fast and powerful return on their money. The most popular initial coin offerings (ICOs) over the last few years are the basis of this optimism, as they have delivered enormous returns. This investor zeal, on the other hand, has the potential to lead people astray.

ICOs are fraught with fraud and con artists seeking to prey on overzealous and poorly educated investors because they are largely unregulated. Funds lost due to fraud or negligence can never be recovered because they are not supervised by financial authorities such as the SEC.

In early September 2017, several governmental and non-governmental bodies reacted to the meteoric rise of ICOs 2017. The People's Bank of China has declared ICOs illegal, deeming them harmful to economic and financial stability.

The Chinese central bank outlawed the use of tokens as currency and forbade banks from providing ICO-related services. As a result, both bitcoin and ethereum prices plummeted, fueling speculation that further cryptocurrency legislation is on the way. The prohibition also applied to offerings that had already been completed. Facebook, Twitter, and Google blocked 8 ICO ads in early 2018.

When it comes to ICOs, there is no assurance that an investor will not become a victim of a scam. Investors should take the following precautions to prevent ICO scams:

Ensure that the project planner can identify their objectives. Whitepapers for successful ICOs are usually easy, understandable, and have specific, concise objectives.

Get to know the programmers. Investors should expect a company launching an ICO to be fully transparent.

Look for the ICO's legal terms and conditions. Since outside regulators rarely monitor this industry, it is up to investors to ensure that any ICO they participate in is legitimate.

Verify the ICO funds are being held in an escrow account. This is a wallet that can only be opened with multiple keys. This can help protect you from scams, particularly if one of the keys is held by a neutral third party.

The HoweyCoin is a cryptocurrency introduced by the Securities and Exchange Commission.

Because of the legal ambiguity under which they operate, ICO operations started to decline drastically in 2019.

The Securities and Exchange Commission of the United States created the HoweyCoin to show small investors the risks of ICOs. The HoweyCoin takes its name from the Howey test, which is used to decide whether an investment is a security. The Howey Test is used to determine whether a transaction is an investment contract when someone invests money in a common enterprise and is led to believe that profits will come solely from the promoter's or a third party's efforts.

Kik, a messaging service that raised $100 million in an unregistered

ICO, was charged with unlawful sale of a security by the SEC.

The SEC has also taken action against Telegram, another messaging app that went public through an initial coin offering.1

According to the SEC, an ICO is similar to an IPO if the underlying token is used to raise funds for a pre-existing company and not operate independently.

An ICO is a form of initial coin offering (ICO)

The amounts raised by the largest projects grew in tandem with the growth of the ICO space. When assessing ICOs, one should consider both the amount of money raised and the return on investment.

ICOs with a high return on investment isn't always the ones who earn the most money and vice versa. Ethereum's initial coin offering (ICO) in 2014 was a forerunner, raising $18 million in 42 days. 15 Due to its advances in decentralized applications, Ethereum has proved to be essential for the ICO space in general (dApps). 16 Ether was initially valued at around $0.67, and as of September 24, 2020, it is trading at $348.99.6.

A two-phase ICO for a firm named Antshares, which was later rebranded as NEO, started in 2015. The ICO's first phase finished in October 2015, and the second phase ran until September 2016. NEO made about $4.5 million during this period. Though it is not one of the most successful ICOs in terms of funds raised, it has given excellent returns to many early investors. The price of NEO was around $0.03 at the time of the ICO, and it peaked at around $187.40.17 18

In terms of total funds raised, ICOs have recently raised considerably more money. Dragon Coin raised $320 million during a one-month ICO that ended in March 2018. 19 More recently, the company behind the EOS platform broke Dragon Coin's record by raising $4 billion in an ICO that lasted a year 20

CHAPTER 8: TECHNICAL ANALYSIS FOR CRYPTOCURRENCY TRADING: THE FUNDAMENTALS

Since the cryptocurrency market is unpredictable, you'll need a trading strategy to keep you on track. Many cryptocurrency traders use technical research to aid in the development of their strategies. This form of study will provide insight into cryptocurrency's past trends, allowing you to forecast where it will go in the future.

Technical Analysis: What Is It and How Does It Work?

You must first grasp what technical analysis is before you can use it in your cryptocurrency trading. Technical forecasting is the process of predicting the future of a business using real-world data. It entails looking at historical data on the cryptocurrencies in question, such as volume and movement.

Fundamental analysis is another popular approach for determining the cryptocurrency's intrinsic value. On the other hand, technical analysis looks at patterns and analytic charting methods to see the crypto's strengths and limitations, holding them in mind for potential patterns. Traders also use technical analysis in more conventional assets such as stocks, currencies, commodities, futures, and forex. Using technical research on all of those properties would be remarkably close to using it on cryptocurrencies.

The Basic Ideas Technical Analysis Is Based On

A few concepts are part of the Dow Theory and serve as a foundation for technical research. To begin with, the theory suggests that market pricing takes into account all factors. That "all" in cryptocurrencies includes present, future, and past demand, legislation, trader expectations, trader awareness of the cryptocurrency, and more. Traders use technical analysis to look at the price to see what it means regarding market sentiment.

When it comes to crypto pricing or patterns, technical research operates under the premise that history repeats itself. Technical analysts use this information to make assumptions about consumer psychology and cryptocurrency.

Technical analysis is often based on the notion that price fluctuations are never random. Rather, these price changes are guided by short- or long-term patterns. When a cryptocurrency follows one pattern, it almost always follows the opposite trend as well. Traders using technical analysis will attempt to isolate these movements to benefit.

In general, technological research is more concerned about what is happening than with why it is happening. Instead of thinking about millions of factors that drive price movements, the emphasis is on supply and demand.

HOW TO READ CANDLESTICK CHARTS

A candlestick chart or graph is the most common form of graph used by crypto traders for technical analysis. It can seem overwhelming at first, but once you get the hang of it, it's pretty simple to comprehend.

Candlestick gets its name from the fact that each plot point on the graph resembles a candlestick. They're red (or pink) or green rectangles with a line coming out of the top or bottom, similar to a candle's wick. The size and line of the candlestick, as well as the color, reveal important details.

The opening and closing prices of the cryptocurrency for that day are at the top and bottom of the main rectangle of the candlestick. The opening price is at the bottom, and the closing price is at the top, indicating that the crypto has increased in value. Green is a good color since the coin's value has risen. The opening price of the crypto is at the top, and the closing price is at the bottom, as shown by red (or pink) candlesticks.

Both ends of the candle will have wicks coming out of it. These are the cryptocurrency's lowest and highest values for the same period. In other words, the wicks indicate how volatile the market is right now.

Getting the Basics Out of Candlestick Charts

Candlestick charts can be used to see how a cryptocurrency performed in the past and make projections for the future. If the wicks are long, for example, this means a highly volatile market. As a result, cryptocurrencies have a higher risk of causing you substantial losses or gains throughout the relevant era. Furthermore, given the market's high uncertainty, this could be corrected tomorrow.

When the candlestick's wick is short, however, it means that the demand might be changing. When the top wick is short, the cryptocurrency's highest price that day was most likely notable in the coin's history. A longer wick at the top suggests that the coin was considerably more costly at some stage during the day before traders profited from selling it. This form of pattern can suggest a bearish market that is about to fall.

A short wick on the bottom means that the coin is still being sold. As a result of the increased availability, the cryptocurrency price is expected to fall even more. On the other hand, a longer wick suggests that the price has previously dipped and that no further decline is anticipated. In other terms, traders want to purchase cryptocurrency at its lowest price, which they believe is now. This might lead to more gains in the future.

UNDERSTANDING AND USING TREND LINES

Trend lines are one of the first elements of technical analysis that traders can learn. Trend lines show the direction in which the cryptocurrency is moving, but determining them needs some study. This is especially valid given the brief existence of cryptocurrencies. Because of this instability, the technical analysis must identify the underlying trend moving up or down among the smaller peaks and lows. Trends can also shift sideways, adding to the complexity. A cryptocurrency with a sideways pattern has not shifted dramatically up or down.

The majority of cryptocurrency trading and monitoring tools will have built-in trend lines. These can be automated, but you can also draw your trend lines for a more precise result. Your forecasts would be more accurate if the trend line is accurate.

The procedure for drawing a precise trend line varies depending on the research software you're using. In most cases, the trend line is drawn directly over the candlestick's lowest price. The line is then approximately extended until it reaches the lowest point of the next candlestick. Make the appropriate changes to ensure you get the same lows for both. You should be able to automatically extend the line from there.

UNDERSTANDING SUPPORT AND RESISTANCE LEVELS

Support and resistance are other important concept to grasp in technical analysis. These are two horizontal lines that you can draw on your trading chart to better understand the cryptocurrency.

The support level is the price at which traders are willing to buy large amounts of cryptocurrency. In other words, there is a lot of demand because traders believe the crypto is undervalued. When the cryptocurrency reaches the support level, there will be a surge in demand, which will usually stop the decline. It can even shift the momentum upward in some cases.

The levels of resistance are the polar opposite. In this case, there is a lot of supply but not a lot of demand. Buyers believe the cryptocurrency is currently overpriced and are hesitant to purchase it. If the cryptocurrency price approaches this resistance level, it will encounter an overabundance of supply, causing the fall price.

Cryptocurrency technical analysts will occasionally notice variations on this. In these situations, buyers may congregate near the support lines, and sellers may sell near the resistance lines. When it comes to lateral movement, this happens more frequently.

A breakout of support or resistance levels in your technical analysis most likely indicates that the current trend is strengthening. If the resistance level becomes the support level, the pattern is strengthened even further. Remember that false breakout can happen, in which case the pattern will remain unchanged. As a result, technical research necessitates the examination of several statistics to identify patterns.

GETTING TO KNOW TRADING VOLUMES

A cryptocurrency's trading volume will help you decide whether or not a pattern is important. A high trading volume usually indicates a major trend that you should pay attention to. Low trading volume, on the other hand, suggests a poor trend that may fade quickly.

If the price of a cryptocurrency falls, check the trading volume to put this information to use. In the decreases, look for low volume, and in the rises, look for higher volume. This would mean that the cryptocurrency is likely to be on a positive trajectory with long-term development. If, on the other hand, the amount during those declines increases, the upward trend will most likely come to an end prematurely. Volume can also provide similar details, but it can provide the opposite in a downtrend.

CHAPTER 9: UNDERSTANDING MARKET CAPITALIZATION

When using technical analysis, the cryptocurrency market cap gives you an idea of a coin's stability. Simply multiply the total circulating supply by the price of each coin to get the market cap. Cryptocurrencies with higher market capitalizations are generally more liquid.

<u>What is the Relative Strength Index (RSI)?</u>

Relative Strength Index, or RSI, metrics are used in most cryptocurrency charting programs. The RSI formula is 100 – (100/(1-RS), with RS equaling the ratio between the average number of days a coin was up and the average number of days it was down. This will be calculated for you automatically by your chosen map, and it will normally be shown under your candlestick chart.

The RSI can range between 0 and 100. RSIs of 30 or less means that the cryptocurrency is currently undervalued and that a price increase is likely. If the RSI approaches or exceeds 70, the cryptocurrency is overbought, and its price will fall.

GETTING TO KNOW MOVING AVERAGES

Moving averages are a form of technical analysis that aids in the detection of trends. The moving average is calculated using the average price of a cryptocurrency over a specified period. A day's moving average is usually calculated using the coin's trading values over the previous 20 days. You can build a line by connecting all of the moving averages and extending them to direct your predictions.

Moving averages of this kind are known as exponential moving averages (EMAs). This estimation is more difficult since the more recent price values are given more weight. In an EMA over 15 days, for example, you might give the most recent five days double the calculation coefficient of the ten days before it.

You may use multiple moving averages, each with a different length of time, to obtain deeper perspectives using moving averages. When a shorter-term moving average crosses over a longer-term one, it could signal the start of a new upward trend.

Selecting Timeframes

You will be able to set your time frames on the price map while you perform your technical analysis. There are various choices, including 15-minute, hourly, four-hour, and regular maps, among many others. Your trading style should determine your period.

Intra-day or short-term traders usually open and close positions within a single trading day. If you fall into this group, you can limit your charting to short time frames. Intraday traders sometimes choose five minutes, 15 minutes, or an hour. You shouldn't use a time frame that's any longer than this.

Long-term traders keep their positions for weeks, months, or even years at a time. Long-term cryptocurrency investors should look at charts that span four hours a day or a week. You may also use hourly charts if you fall into this category, but this is less popular.

Use a combination of technical analysis and other methods.

When trading cryptocurrencies, you can never focus solely on technical analysis. It's best not to rely solely on one type of research because this will only provide you with limited knowledge. Technical research alone can not provide insight into sentient or news, all of which are fundamental analyses. This is especially troublesome in cryptocurrency trading since factors such as mining hash and legislation can have a huge effect on a coin's price, but technical analysis ignores them.

Technical research may provide cryptocurrency traders with insight into a cryptocurrency's history, allowing them to make more accurate forecasts in the future. Most charting software includes various technical analysis resources, which you can complement with your research. Often strive to incorporate technical analysis with other approaches for the best results.

CHAPTER 10: HOW MUCH SHOULD YOU INVEST- CRYPTOCURRENCY ASSET ALLOCATION

Overall, some argue that investing in ICOs isn't investing at all but just pure speculation and that it's better to wait until the coins have gone public after the ICO. I agree with the first part of that argument – investing in a brand new startup that hasn't even developed a product at the dawn of a new technological revolution is speculative. I believe that you can look at the ones that have gone public because they are more likely to not be scams.

But I don't think that's what we should be doing. In terms of asset allocation, I assume that a small portion of your portfolio should be invested in ICOs because the returns could be enormous. So, what is a good percentage to aim for? Of course, how old you are, how much risk you are willing to take, and how aggressive/conservative you want to be will all influence your decision. However, it is as follows for me:

In terms of asset allocation, I intend to invest 5% of my resources in initial coin offerings (ICOs).

The explanation is that we don't know:

1. The direction in which this industry is going.

2. Which Initial Coin Offerings (ICOs) will be popular.

As a result, investing in ICOs is HIGHLY RISKY.

Nonetheless, I'm still willing to contribute a small sum each month, say £500+. I want to spread my risk through at least 20 separate ICOs. I'll put more in if I've met the people and have a positive impression of them, or if the white paper makes a lot of sense and is solving a problem, and the team is on board.

To construct the required solution So, if I invested £10,000 in 20 of them and they all failed, but one of them blew up, I'd gamble £10,000 to make £50,000 or more.

For instance, I might put money into:

Investing 0.5 percent of my money in an ICO, I'm not sure about but want to be a part of because I don't want to miss out.

I'm willing to put 1-1.5 percent of my money into an ICO that I believe in.

2.5-5% of my resources into an ICO for which I have a strong feeling about the issue, solution, and team.

I've only ever put 12.5 percent of my crypto resources into one ICO. This was at the start of my journey, and in retrospect, it was an excessive asset distribution.

Let's take a look at how this works:

25% = £2,500 into the top two Ethereum/Bitcoin exchanges.

40% = £4,000 invested in well-known coins, such as the top 20.

20% = £2,000 into up-and-coming coins, i.e., coins that aren't in the top 20 but are rapidly increasing.

10% = £1,000 invested in new coins that have been listed on an exchange.

Investing 5% of your income = £500 in ICOs.

100% Total

This is merely a suggestion for what I'm doing; you must devise the system that works for you.

Keep in mind that this 100 percent represents the entire amount of my pot that I have set aside for cryptocurrencies. Because cryptocurrencies are speculative, this '100%' should not account for more than 10% of your overall portfolio. Even if you lost 100% of your money, you would only have lost 10% of your portfolio. Again, none of us knows where cryptocurrencies will go in the future.

DOES INVESTING IN CRYPTOCURRENCIES HAVE ANY DISADVANTAGES?

"Where there's blockchain, there's also a lot of nonsense."

Cryptocurrencies, especially initial coin offerings (ICOs), have several disadvantages. Since this is a brand-new and unregulated industry, you would not be paid if you are hacked, and your Bitcoins are stolen. Also, new coin releases are on the rise, and no one knows which ones will fade away and which ones will stick around. Price fluctuations of 30% or more up or down in a single day are not unusual due to this uncertainty. As a result, just spend money that you are prepared to risk right now. In general, there are four drawbacks of cryptocurrencies. There is a general lack of knowledge about this digital currency. Furthermore, by using it, there is a minimum level of security and assurance. It is bound to encounter various technical flaws because it is primarily operated online, and it is still in development.

1. Bitcoin is a difficult concept to grasp.

The majority of people are still unaware of digital currencies and their potential. This is similar to how people reacted to credit cards when they were first revealed and reacted to cryptocurrency. People wouldn't have believed it possible back then to pay for things with a card, let alone a whole new digital currency.

People are wary of it because it is different and does not directly involve cash, and they constantly question its efficacy. It also necessitates online access to function. Some people find the idea of paying for things or transferring money online convenient, and it is catching on, but others remain skeptical.

To make cryptocurrency more acceptable in our society, people must be educated about it and incorporate it into their daily lives. Learning a whole new world of currency, on the other hand, takes a lot of time and effort. Most people would think it isn't worth their time because it isn't well-known.

Even though some businesses accept Bitcoins, the list is relatively small when compared to traditional currencies. This is most likely due to a lack of understanding. Customers and businesses both need to be educated. Consider having to teach your customers a new method of payment. This will necessitate more time and effort.

2. There is a lack of customer security and assurance.

Central Banks govern the authority of a nation's money in the case of conventional currency. Without protest and rejection, no higher authority can decide that they no longer want to trade in their country's currency. Procedures must be followed, documents must be filed, approvals must be granted, and many other protocols must be followed.

That is not the case with our digital currency, however. Because a central bank does not govern Bitcoin, no one can guarantee its minimum value.

If a large group of merchants decides to simply 'discard' Bitcoins and leave the system, the value of Bitcoin, for example, will plummet dramatically. Other users who have invested thousands of dollars in Bitcoins will undoubtedly suffer a significant loss due to this. There is no one to contact to report these losses, and there are no rules in place to help compensate them.

Another example is if you were charged but did not receive your online movie tickets or flight tickets, you can always contact your bank service provider or go to a physical bank to file a complaint. If you pay with a Visa card and show that you did not receive the service, the credit card company will refund your money. I recall paying £2,000 for a never-delivered course – the guy simply took our money and ran. Because we used their credit card, Visa compensated us fully. I was both impressed and horrified at the time, as I can imagine many people making false claims.

With cryptocurrency, this is not the case. First and foremost, there is no bank to negotiate with and assist you with this currency. There is no phone number or email address to call to request a callback.

So, if you bought something with Bitcoins and the merchant didn't send it to you, there's nothing you can do to get a refund or reverse the transaction. You are unable to file a complaint with the police or any other relevant authority.

In most cases, cryptocurrency transactions are irreversible. You can't get your money back once you've sent it to someone's address. So double-check that you're sending coins to the correct address and in the correct currency.

As a result, the appeal of Bitcoin's decentralized system is a double-edged sword.

3. Technical shortcomings

When online banking first became popular, there was always the risk of a server outage, a power outage, or even hardware lags.

If your hard drive crashes and your wallet file becomes corrupted, your Bitcoin will be lost forever, similar to data corruption or virus infections. You won't be able to restore it, and those "coins" will become "orphaned" in the system.

So, to avoid this from happening, always create a backup.

4. The industry is also in its early stages.

Things are vulnerable to many threats as they are still developing. Several unfinished features can be enhanced, but completing them takes longer, particularly if they do not have a physical shape.

Although transfers are made electronically, and we don't see the real money being moved from one account to another, we still end up with physical cash at the end of the day with conventional currency. We can buy items in shops, both physically and online, using physical cash.

Since cryptocurrency has no physical nature, i.e., we will never carry physical cash, its use is restricted.

In the end, it is more often than not – and I hope this changes soon – necessary to convert Bitcoin to traditional currency to benefit from its value.

THE FUTURE OF CRYPTOCURRENCY

Some of the current limitations of cryptocurrencies, such as the fact that a computer crash can erase one's digital fortune or a virtual vault can be ransacked by a hacker, may be overcome in the future thanks to technological advancements. What will be more difficult to overcome is the fundamental paradox that plagues cryptocurrencies: the more popular they become, the more regulation and government scrutiny they are likely to face, eroding the fundamental premise for their existence.

While the number of merchants accepting cryptocurrencies has steadily grown, they remain a small minority. To gain widespread acceptance, cryptocurrencies must first gain consumer acceptance. However, most people, except the technologically savvy, will be put off by their relative complexity compared to traditional currencies.

A cryptocurrency that aspires to join the mainstream financial system may be required to meet various requirements. It would have to be mathematically complex (to avoid fraud and hacker attacks) but simple to understand for consumers; decentralized but with adequate consumer safeguards and protection; and maintain user anonymity without being used for tax evasion, money laundering, or other nefarious activities. Is it possible that the most popular cryptocurrency in a few years will have characteristics that fall somewhere between heavily-regulated fiat currencies and today's cryptocurrencies, given these difficult criteria to meet? While that possibility appears remote, there is little doubt that as the most popular cryptocurrency at the moment, Bitcoin's success (or lack thereof) in dealing with the challenges it faces will have a significant impact on the fortunes of other cryptocurrencies in the years ahead.

Should You Invest in Cryptocurrencies?

If you're thinking about investing in cryptocurrencies, you should approach it like any other high-risk venture. To put it another way, accept the possibility of losing the majority, if not all, of your investment. As previously stated, a cryptocurrency's intrinsic value is determined by the price a buyer is willing to pay for it at any given time. As a result, it is extremely vulnerable to large price swings, increasing the risk of losing an investor. For example, on April 11, 2013, Bitcoin dropped from $260 to around $130 in six hours.18 If you can't handle that kind of volatility, look for other options. While opinions on the merits of Bitcoin as an investment remain sharply divided – supporters point to its limited supply and growing usage as value drivers, while detractors see it as just another speculative bubble – this is one debate that a conservative investor would do well to steer clear of.

The rise of Bitcoin has sparked a discussion about its and other cryptocurrencies' futures. Despite recent issues, Bitcoin's success since its launch in 2009 has sparked the development of alternative cryptocurrencies such as Etherium, Litecoin, and Ripple. A cryptocurrency that aspires to join the mainstream financial system would have to meet a variety of requirements. While that possibility appears remote, it is undeniable that Bitcoin's success or failure in dealing with the challenges it faces will have a significant impact on the fortunes of other cryptocurrencies in the years ahead.

CONCLUSION

Cryptocurrency is unquestionably the currency of the future. Cryptocurrency has numerous advantages, including the fact that it is based on Blockchain technology, which allows it to: Easy to monitor, Tamper proof, Transparent and Quick (in terms of transactions)

Consumers must understand how this currency is developing and whether their country supports or opposes it. Laws and the current financial structure could change overnight, bringing with them completely new modes of payment and earning!

BITCOIN TRADING FOR BEGINNERS

The Ultimate Simple Guide to Understand Easily How to Start Investing and Buy Bitcoins Safely. Learn Basic and Advanced Strategy to Make a Passive Income

Andrew Douglas

INTRODUCTION

Bitcoin is a digital currency that was first introduced in January of 2009. It is based on ideas presented in a whitepaper by Satoshi Nakamoto, a mysterious and pseudonymous figure. The identity of the person or people behind the technology is still unknown. Bitcoin promises lower transaction costs than conventional online payment methods, and it is run by a decentralized authority, unlike government-issued currencies.

Bitcoin is a type of cryptocurrency. There are no physical bitcoins; instead, balances are kept on a public ledger that anyone can see. A vast amount of computational power is used to verify all bitcoin transactions. Individual bitcoins are not valuable as commodities since they are not distributed or guaranteed by any banks or governments. Although it is not legal tender, Bitcoin is extremely popular and has sparked hundreds of other cryptocurrencies known as altcoins. "BTC" is a common abbreviation for Bitcoin.

The bitcoin system is a collection of computers (also known as "nodes" or "miners") that run bitcoin's code and store its blockchain. A blockchain can be thought of as a series of blocks metaphorically. Each block contains a set of transactions. No one can cheat the system because all computers running the blockchain have the same list of blocks and transactions and can see all new blocks being filled with new bitcoin transactions transparently.

These transactions can be seen by anyone, whether or not they run a bitcoin "node." A bad actor will need to operate 51 percent of the computing power that makes up bitcoin to achieve a nefarious act. As of January 2021, Bitcoin had about 12,000 nodes, and this number is increasing, making quite an attack quite unlikely.

However, if an attack were to occur, bitcoin miners—those who participated in the bitcoin network with their computers—would most likely fork to a new blockchain, making the bad actor's effort put forth to achieve the attack a waste.

Public and private "keys," which are long strings of letters and numbers and connected by the mathematical encryption algorithm used to generate them, are used to keep track of bitcoin token balances. The public key (which is similar to a bank account number) serves as the made public's address and to which others may send bitcoins.

The private key (comparable to an ATM PIN) is intended to be kept private and is only used to authorize bitcoin transactions. A bitcoin wallet, a physical or digital device that enables bitcoin trading and allows users to monitor ownership of coins, should not be confused with bitcoin keys. The term "wallet" is misleading because bitcoin is never held "in" a wallet but rather decentralized on a blockchain.

CHAPTER 1: HOW TO PURCHASE BITCOIN

Investing in Bitcoin may seem difficult initially, but it becomes much simpler once you break it down into stages. Purchasing Bitcoin is becoming easier by the day, and the trustworthiness of exchanges and wallets is increasing.

• Bitcoin's value stems from its use as a store of value and payment mechanism and its limited supply and low inflation.
• While it is almost impossible to hack Bitcoin itself, your wallet or exchange account can be hacked. This is why proper storage and security procedures are important.
• All that is needed to invest or trade Bitcoin is an account on an exchange, though additional safe storage practices are recommended.

Before You Get Started

Several items are required for any aspiring Bitcoin investor. You'll need a cryptocurrency exchange account, personal identity documents, a secure Internet connection, and a payment system if you're using a Know Your Customer (KYC) network. Separating your wallet from your exchange account is also a good idea. This route accepts bank accounts, debit cards, and credit cards as payment types. Specialized ATMs and peer-to-peer (P2P) exchanges are also options for getting Bitcoin. However, as of early 2020, Bitcoin ATMs increasingly required government-issued identification.

To buy bitcoin, you'll need a digital wallet, personal identification documents, a secure internet connection, a cryptocurrency exchange, and a method of payment.

Privacy and security are major concerns for Bitcoin investors. Even if there are no Bitcoins, boasting about large holdings is usually not a good idea. Anyone who gets their hands on the private key to a Bitcoin public address can approve transactions. Although private keys should be kept private, criminals may try to steal them if they learn large holdings. Keep in mind that everybody can use the balance of a public address device. As a result, keeping large investments at public addresses that aren't linked to the ones used for transactions is a good idea.

The blockchain's transaction history is accessible to anyone, including you. Personal information about users is not publicly reported on the blockchain, even though transactions are. Only a user's public key appears next to a Bitcoin blockchain transaction, making transactions private but not anonymous. In some respects, bitcoin transactions are easier and more traceable than cash, but they can also be used anonymously.

This is a significant distinction. According to international researchers and the FBI, Bitcoin blockchain transfers to users' other online accounts, such as digital wallets, can be tracked. Anyone who wants to open a Coinbase account, for example, must provide identification. When that person purchases Bitcoin, it is linked to their name. If they send it to another wallet, it can be traced back to the Coinbase transaction connected to the account holder's name. Since Bitcoin is legal in the United States and most developed countries, many investors should be unconcerned.

Step 1: Choose an Exchange

Signing up for a cryptocurrency exchange allows you to buy, sell, and keep cryptocurrency. Users are generally advised to use an exchange to deposit their cryptocurrency into a personal wallet for safekeeping. On some exchanges and brokerage sites, this is prohibited. For those who trade Bitcoin or other cryptocurrencies regularly, this feature may be irrelevant.

Exchanges for cryptocurrencies come in a variety of shapes and sizes. Some exchanges allow users to remain anonymous and do not require them to enter personal information due to the decentralization and individual autonomy ethos of Bitcoin. The exchanges that make this possible are usually self-contained and decentralized, which means there is no single point of control. To put it another way, if a regulatory body suspects criminal activity, there is no CEO and no individual or group to investigate.

Although these programs can be used for malicious purposes, they also provide services to the unbanked. This category includes refugees and those who live in countries with little or no government or banking infrastructure. To open a bank or investment account, state identification is required. Some argue that because unbanked people already have a way to save money and use it to get out of poverty, these programs' benefits outweigh the risk of illicit use.

Currently, the most widely used types of exchanges are not decentralized and require KYC. In the United States, these exchanges include Kraken, Coinbase, Gemini, and Binance U.S., to name a few. The number of features offered by each of these exchanges has significantly increased. Coinbase, Kraken, and Gemini all offer Bitcoin and a growing number of altcoins. These three methods are arguably the most straightforward in the entire industry for getting started with cryptocurrency. Binance is geared for the more seasoned trader, with more advanced trading features and a wide range of altcoins.

It's important to use safe internet practices when opening a cryptocurrency exchange account. This requires the use of two-factor authentication and the development of a unique and long password containing a mix of lowercase, capitalized, special, and numeric characters.

Step 2: Integrate Your Exchange with a Payment Method

Once you've decided on a program, you'll need to collect your records. These could include images of a driver's license, your social security number, as well as information about your employer and source of funds, depending on the exchange. The knowledge you'll need is likely to be determined by the area you reside in and the laws that govern it. The procedure is similar to that of opening a traditional brokerage account.

You can buy and sell bitcoin and deposit the money directly into your bank account by connecting your wallet to your bank account.

After the exchange has checked your identity and legitimacy, you can now connect a payment option. You may connect your bank account or a debit or credit card to the exchanges mentioned above directly.

While it is possible to purchase cryptocurrency with a credit card, it is usually advised against doing so due to cryptocurrencies' volatility.

Although Bitcoin is legal in the United States, some banks are skeptical of the concept and may decline to make deposits to cryptocurrency-related websites or exchanges. While most banks accept these deposits, double-check that your bank accepts deposits at the exchange you want to use.

Similar fees apply to deposits made with a checking account, debit card, or credit card. For example, Coinbase charges 1.49 percent for bank accounts and 3.99 percent for debit and credit cards, making it a good exchange for newcomers. Before deciding on an exchange or which payment option is best for you, it's critical to understand the fees associated with each payment option.

Step 3: Make a Purchase

After choosing an exchange and connecting a payment form, you can now buy Bitcoin and other cryptocurrencies. In recent years, cryptocurrency and cryptocurrency exchanges have grown in popularity. Exchanges have grown dramatically in terms of liquidity and feature set. What was once considered a scam or questionable has grown into something trustworthy and legitimate.

Cryptocurrency exchanges have advanced to the point that they now provide almost identical features to their stock brokerage counterparts. Once you've found an exchange and connected a payment method, you're ready to go.

Cryptocurrency exchanges also offer a wide range of order forms and investment options. Market and cap requests are accepted by almost every cryptocurrency exchange, and some also accept stop-loss orders. Of the exchanges mentioned above, Kraken has the most order types. On Kraken, you can place market, cap, stop-loss, stop-limit, and take-profit limit orders.

Aside from various order types, exchanges frequently offer clients the option of setting up recurring investments, which allow them to dollar cost average into their chosen investments. Coinbase, for example, lets users schedule transactions for the next day, week, or month. To buy Bitcoin or other cryptocurrencies, all you have to do is open an account on a cryptocurrency exchange. Still, there are a few other steps to take for added security and safety.

Step 4: Proper Storage

Bitcoin and other cryptocurrency wallets are a safe way to keep digital assets. Keeping your cryptocurrency in your wallet rather than on an exchange means that your funds' private key is only accessible to you. It also enables you to store funds outside of an exchange, lowering the risk of your funds being stolen if the exchange is compromised.

Bitcoins are a form of digital currency that must be stored in a digital wallet.

Although most exchanges offer wallets to their users, protection is not their top priority. We don't recommend using an exchange wallet for massive or long-term cryptocurrency holdings.

Some wallets come with a larger number of options than others. Some only accept Bitcoin, while others accept several altcoins. You can also swap one token for another in certain wallets.

When it comes to choosing a Bitcoin wallet, you have a lot of options. The first thing you can learn about crypto wallets is the difference between hot wallets (online wallets) and cold wallets (paper or hardware wallets).

COLD WALLETS

A cold wallet is simply a wallet that is not linked to the internet and poses a significantly lower risk of being hacked. These wallets are also known as hardware wallets or offline wallets.

These wallets store a user's private key on a device that isn't connected to the internet, and they can have software that runs in the background so that the user can access their portfolio without risking their private key. Offline, a paper wallet is also the safest place to store cryptocurrency. A paper wallet can be printed from several different websites. It then produces public and private keys, which you can print out. You can only get cryptocurrency from these addresses if you have the private key on a piece of paper. Many people laminate these paper wallets and store them in a safe deposit box at their bank or in their home safe. These wallets are best for high security and long-term investments because you can't easily sell or swap Bitcoin stored in them.

A hardware wallet is a form of cold wallet that is more widely used. A hardware wallet is a device that stores a user's private keys on the internet on a USB drive. This has many advantages over hot wallets, including the fact that it is immune to viruses on the user's computer. With hardware wallets, your private keys never come into touch with your network-connected computer or potentially compromised applications. These devices are also open source, enabling the world to vote on their protection rather than a company declaring it safe to use.

The best place to store Bitcoin and other cryptocurrencies are in a cold wallet. Setting them up, on the other hand, normally necessitates a little more experience.

A smart way to set up your wallets is to have three of them: a buying and selling exchange account, a hot wallet for small to medium amounts of crypto you want to trade or sell, and a cold hardware wallet long-term storage of larger holdings.

HOT WALLETS

"Cold" wallets are another term for online wallets. Hot wallets are digital wallets that operate on internet-connected devices such as laptops, smartphones, and tablets. Since these wallets produce the private keys to your coins on these internet-connected devices, this may pose a risk. While a hot wallet can be very useful for quickly accessing and transacting with your money, storing your private key on an internet-connected computer makes it more vulnerable to hacking.

While it might seem impossible, people who use these hot wallets without sufficient security risk getting their funds stolen. This is a natural occurrence that can manifest itself in several ways. It's not a good idea, for example, to brag about how much Bitcoin you have on a public forum like Reddit while using little to no security and keeping it in a hot wallet. These wallets, however, can be made to be secure if precautions are taken. Strong passwords, two-factor authentication, and secure internet browsing should all be needed.

These wallets are best for storing small amounts of bitcoin or cryptocurrencies that you are actively trading on an exchange. A hot wallet works in the same way as a checking account. According to traditional financial wisdom, you can keep just your discretionary money in a bank account and invest the remainder in savings or other investment vehicles. The same can be said for hot wallets. Hot wallets include mobile, laptop, network, and exchange account custody wallets.

As previously mentioned, exchange wallets are custodial accounts provided by the exchange. This wallet type owner does not have access to the private key to the cryptocurrency deposited in this wallet. If the exchange was hacked or if your account was compromised, your funds would be lost. The phrase "not your key, not your coin" is frequently heard in cryptocurrency forums and groups.

CHAPTER 2: WALLET FOR BITCOIN

What is a Bitcoin Wallet, and How does it work ?

A Bitcoin wallet is a piece of software that stores Bitcoins. Bitcoins are not technically processed anywhere. Every person with a balance in a Bitcoin wallet has a private key (secret number) that corresponds to its Bitcoin address. Bitcoin wallets allow users to send and receive Bitcoins while also granting them ownership of their Bitcoin balance. Bitcoin wallets come in a variety of shapes and sizes. Desktop, tablet, internet, and hardware are the four major categories.

•   A Bitcoin wallet is a software program for storing and exchanging Bitcoins rather than a physical object.

•   A private key protects wallets. The key corresponds to the wallet's address.

•   Laptop, tablet, internet, and hardware are the four styles of Bitcoin wallets.

Getting to Know Bitcoin Wallets

A digital wallet is another name for a Bitcoin wallet. A trader must first create a digital wallet to exchange Bitcoins. A Bitcoin wallet works in the same way as a physical wallet. Instead of physical currency, the wallet stores relevant data such as the encrypted private key used to access Bitcoin addresses and complete transactions. Desktop, tablet, internet, and hardware wallets are examples of Bitcoin wallets.

Desktop Wallets

Desktop wallets are mounted on a device and give the user full control over the wallet. Desktop wallets serve as a user's address for sending and receiving Bitcoins. They also offer the user the option of storing a private key. Bitcoin Core, MultiBit, Armory, Hive OS X, and Electrum are a few well-known desktop wallets.

Mobile Wallets

Mobile wallets are similar to desktop wallets in terms of functionality. Mobile wallets allow "touch-to-pay" and the scanning of a Q.R. code with near field communication (NFC) in physical stores. Mobile wallets include Bitcoin Wallet, Hive Android, and Mycelium Bitcoin Wallet. Bitcoin wallets are usually compatible with either the iOS or Android operating systems. Since there is a lot of malware masquerading as Bitcoin wallets, it's best to do some research before deciding which one to use.

Web Wallets

Web wallets enable users to access Bitcoins from any browser or mobile device. Since your private keys are stored online, you must choose your web wallet carefully. Famous web wallet providers include Coinbase and Blockchain.

Hardware Wallets

Hardware wallets, which store Bitcoins on a physical piece of equipment normally plugged into a computer via a USB port, are by far the most stable form of Bitcoin wallet. They are virtually resistant to virus attacks, and there have been few reports of Bitcoin theft. These are the only Bitcoin wallets that aren't secure, costing anywhere from $100 to $200.

Special Security Considerations for Wallets

Bitcoin wallets are high-value targets for hackers, so keeping them secure is important. Encrypting the wallet with a strong password and selecting a cold storage choice, which means storing Bitcoins offline, are two precautions. It's also a good idea to back up your desktop and mobile wallets regularly, as problems with the wallet software on your computer or mobile device could wipe out your assets.

CHAPTER 3: BUY BITCOIN ANYWHERE IN THE WORLD

There are various ways to buy Bitcoin in almost every country, including gift cards, bitcoin ATMs, local traders, brokers, and exchanges: This Chapter discusses how to purchase Bitcoin from any location on the planet.

Perhaps you've heard of Bitcoin, the bizarre cryptocurrency. The holy grail of Fintech, the future of finance, the payment revolution, the digital gold, the slayer of capital controls You may now be curious to learn more. The best way to learn is to do it yourself. Purchase a Bitcoin, use it to make a payment, save it in your digital wallet, and watch the price rise or fall. However, where do you get it? And how do you do it?

For many people, purchasing their first Bitcoin is a frightening experience. It appears to be extremely difficult. However, this is not the case. There are numerous options for purchasing your first Bitcoin quickly, conveniently, and comfortably.

Which one is the best is determined by your location and personal preferences.

TLDR:
1. Purchase Bitcoin with regular fiat currency.
2. If you have a wallet, you may purchase Bitcoins on a Bitcoin exchange using a conventional payment system such as a credit card, bank transfer (ACH), debit card, interact, or E-transfer.
3. After that, the Bitcoins are moved to your cryptocurrency

wallet.

However, before deciding on the best way to buy your first Bitcoin, you should consider the following factors:

- How much personal information are you willing to share?
- How would you like to pay?
- Where do you call home?

You should be able to easily determine which platform best suits your needs based on these factors.

This guide begins by outlining the choices for disclosing private information (or not disclosing it) and the payment methods available to you. The guide goes into the most popular ways to buy Bitcoin and an overview of many exchanges in various countries.

HOW TO PURCHASE BITCOIN FROM ANYWHERE ON THE WORLD

Private Information

Bitcoin is a financial instrument, and as such, most jurisdictions regulate it. Anti-Money-Laundering (AML) regulations are almost universally applied to websites selling Bitcoins or allowing users to buy and sell Bitcoins. To verify its customers' identity, most of these platforms must implement Know Your Customer (KYC) laws.

Since Bitcoin transactions are saved publicly available on the blockchain and can be traced back, the number of personal details you reveal while purchasing Bitcoins can have significant privacy implications.

There are many levels of KYC, each requiring you to reveal more personal details. The following is a list of grades, starting with the lowest:

- No Know Your Customer (KYC): If you don't have a KYC, the network or the Bitcoin seller does not know who you are. You don't need to display identification and pay with cash, Moneygram, Paysafecard, or Western Union. In some jurisdictions, buying Bitcoin without KYC is possible – for example, through P2P marketplaces such as LocalBitcoins, ATMs, or Gift Cards – but it is typically more costly than other alternatives.

- KYC Light: This KYC level uses your payment channel and/or phone numbers to identify you. Payment providers know your identity whether you pay through your bank account, PayPal, credit card, or another popular payment method. With KYC Light, you can buy a limited amount of Bitcoins on most sites, including direct exchanges, trading platforms, and marketplaces.

• Full KYC: In addition to using your phone number and bank account to check your identity, Full KYC requires you to have documents that prove your identity. A passport, an I.D. card, a driver's license, a utility bill, or a combination of all of these may be used. Some platforms require a notary or a trustworthy third party, such as your bank, to approve your identity documents; others are happy if you upload a photo of yourself holding your I.D. card or participate in the video verification process. There is typically no way around Full KYC if you want to spend significant sums of money or trade on exchanges.

WHAT IS THE BEST METHOD FOR PURCHASING BITCOIN?

Bitcoin is currency, but it can only be purchased by sending money to someone else. The more advanced your country's financial system is, and the better your country's financial system is, the easier it is to trade your money for Bitcoins.

The most significant impediment to Bitcoin trading is the movement of old fiat currency. Your Bitcoin will be acquired slowly and at a high cost if you use a slow and costly payment method. You can buy Bitcoins quickly if you use a fast channel.

Here's a partial, non-exhaustive list of popular ways to pay for Bitcoin:

• **Bank transfer**: Almost everybody is familiar with the good old Bank transfer. Typically, you send money to a Bitcoin seller and receive Bitcoins after the payments are completed using online banking. This takes 1-3 days in most countries. Direct debiting is not commonly recognized. Bank transfers are the only method of payment accepted by the majority of exchange platforms.

• **Credit Card**: Credit cards are one of the most widely used payment methods. However, credit cards are accepted by only a few direct commercial vendors. The explanation for this is that Bitcoin transactions cannot be reversed, whereas credit card transactions can. Vendors who accept credit cards have suffered losses as a result of this. Vendors often run the risk of people purchasing Bitcoin with stolen credit cards. Benefit from stolen credit card numbers with Bitcoins and use algorithms to reduce the danger.

• **PayPal:** Although a few sites support PayPal, most of them oppose it due to the same issues that credit cards have: PayPal transactions are easily reversed. The vendor can lose if this occurs after the buyer has moved the purchased Bitcoin to another wallet. This is why trading Bitcoins on eBay is a bad idea. However, some sites, including credit cards, accept PayPal.

• **Other Payment Channels**: (Sofort, iDeal, Skrill, etc.): Payment providers abound in the world of commerce. There are hundreds of them in the E.U. alone. A large number of direct exchanges supports a diverse selection of them. If you use a common supplier, such as Sofort in Germany or iDeal in the Netherlands, your domestic direct exchange is likely to accept it.

• **Private Payment Channels** (Cash, Western Union, Paysafecard, etc.): Most commercial platforms do not accept these payment methods. There are very few trading sites and almost certainly no direct exchanges that accept these payments. On p2p marketplaces, however, you will frequently find a seller who accepts cash or other private payment methods. An ATM where you can buy Bitcoins with cash might also be a good option.

WHAT IS THE MOST COST-EFFECTIVE METHOD OF PURCHASING BITCOIN?

We're getting closer to acquiring your Bitcoin now. In this section of our guide, we'll show you a few popular models for converting fiat money to digital cash – in Bitcoin. Each model has its own set of benefits and drawbacks.

• **Bitcoin ATM:** A Bitcoin ATM is perhaps the simplest and most private way to obtain Bitcoins. These machines where you can get money with your passport, you're familiar with them. Some companies, such as Lamassu, make Bitcoin ATMs where you can buy Bitcoin with cash. These devices' operators may use various KYC rules, ranging from cell phone authentication to biometric methods if they so choose. You will find a global map of these devices on Coin-ATM-Radar.com. Another type of ATM simply uses an existing ATM network to sell Bitcoins, such as those found in banks or train stations. This has been achieved in Switzerland, Ukraine, and Spain, for example. The majority of ATMs charge a fee of 3-6 percent or even more.

• **Gift Cards/Vouchers:** Another simple way to purchase Bitcoins is with a gift card or voucher. You go to a kiosk or another store and purchase a gift card or a voucher, then go to a website and enter the code on the card to get your Bitcoin. This approach is used in Austria, Mexico, and South Korea, among other places. Gift cards, like ATMs, are notorious for charging exorbitant fees.

• **Direct commercial exchanges/brokers:** These vendors are similar to the exchange offices found in airports, but they are interactive. They use an exchange to purchase Bitcoins and then sell them to customers. You go to a website, choose your payment method, pay, and receive Bitcoins at the platform's fixed rates. Most of these platforms require you to have your wallet, but others, such as Coinbase and Circle, allow you to save and spend your Bitcoins using a wallet they offer. Since such sites accept a wide range of payment methods, including credit cards and PayPal, they can be the quickest and most convenient way for newcomers to purchase their first Bitcoin. The fees for direct commercial exchanges range from 1% to 5%. Any of them benefit from the difference between buying and selling prices. Most charge additional fees for such payment methods, such as credit cards.

• **P2P-Marketplaces:** Buyers and sellers of Bitcoin meet and trade on P2P-marketplaces. The fees on these markets are modest, ranging from 0 to 1%; the spread is determined by the market's liquidity and the payment channel. You can take and make a bid, unlike direct: You decide on a price and then wait for someone to sell you a Bitcoin. This allows you to buy vast quantities of Bitcoin for relatively low prices. LocalBitcoins is the most well-known P2P marketplace. This global marketplace accepts various currencies and allows buyers and sellers to choose their preferred payment method. It's often used to encourage anonymous transactions, often at exorbitant rates. Bitcoin.de, the Eurozone's largest peer-to-peer (P2P) market, has strong liquidity and is a convenient way to convert Euro to Bitcoin. Bitsquare, a fully decentralized market that is nothing more than software that links people, is the third well-known P2P market.

• **Trading platforms:** Whether you want to buy large quantities of Bitcoin at low rates daily or trade with Bitcoins, you'll probably need an exchange platform. Exchanges serve as escrow for their customers, storing both Bitcoin and fiat money on their behalf. You can place your buy or sell orders here, and the exchanges' trading engine compiles these orders and offers from buyers and sellers and executes trades. Frequently, exchanges offer more trading options, such as margin trading. Fees and spreads are usually minimal. However, opening an account on an exchange can be difficult since it necessitates sharing personal details and trusting the exchange with your funds.

Exchanges, wallets, and banks have all been warned about.

Regardless of the proof of identity criteria, keep in mind that exchanges and wallets do not provide the same security level as banks.

For example, if the exchange goes out of business or is hacked, as was the case with the notorious failed exchange Mt Gox, there is sometimes no or restricted protection for your account.

In certain parts of the world, Bitcoin is not recognized as a legal tender, and authorities are sometimes at a loss regarding how to respond to robberies. Any larger exchanges have replaced customer funds after a fraud from the exchange, but they are not legally obligated to do so at this time.

WHAT IS THE BEST WAY TO BUY BITCOIN IN YOUR COUNTRY?

Worldwide: You can use local bitcoins, BitSquare, or Bitcoin ATMs almost anywhere on the planet. Although these are viable options, it is worthwhile to investigate other options available in your region.

NORTH AMERICA
The United States and Canada are two of the most famous Bitcoin markets. Buyers can purchase Bitcoins using several methods. Aside from LocalBitcoins and ATMs, direct vendors Coinbase, Circle, India Coin, the P2P-market Paxful, and the exchange Kraken are available in both countries.

UNITED STATES OF AMERICA
* Direct Exchanges: Two main sites, Coinbase and Kraken,

make it simple to buy Bitcoins with low fees and store them in an online wallet. Both services support credit cards and bank transfers. Indacoin is another direct exchange network, but it lacks an integrated wallet. Another alternative, Expresscoin, allows you to buy Bitcoins with cash using Billpay.

• <u>P2P-Markets</u>: In addition to LocalBitcoins and Bitsquare, P2P-markets Bitquick and Paxful are available to consumers in the United States. On Bitquick, you pay by depositing cash into the seller's bank account; on Paxful, the seller can select from various payment methods, including PayPal, Western Union, credit and debit cards, gift cards, and more. Although Paxful's rates are normally very high, Bitquick charges a 2% fee.

• <u>Exchanges</u>: There are a few platforms to choose from if you want to buy Bitcoins with a Dollar on an exchange. Bitstamp, Coinbase's GDAX, and Bitfinex are the most common exchanges, followed by BTC-E, Kraken, and Gemini. While most exchanges only support bank transfers, BTC-E allows users to finance their accounts using credit cards and other payment providers such as PerfectMoney, Paysafecards, and others.

CANADA

• <u>Direct</u>: Both Kraken and Coinbase accept Canadian customers who can purchase Bitcoins using a bank transfer or a credit card and store them in the platform's online wallet. Customers from Canada may also use Indacoin. QuickBT and canadianbitcoins.com, for example, are websites where you can directly purchase Bitcoins for up to 150 Canadian Dollars using various payment methods such as INTERAC® Online and Flexepin Vouchers. Canadianbitcoin.com also accepts cash payments in person or by deposit.

• <u>P2P</u>: Canadian customers can purchase Bitcoins on foreign P2P markets such as Paxful and LocalBitcoin.

• <u>Exchange</u>: Canadian Dollars can be traded on some exchanges. The most well-known examples are Kraken and CoinSquare.

SOUTH AND CENTRAL AMERICA

Other than North America, Middle and South America were only recently introduced to Bitcoins, mainly in 2014/2015. Since most exchanges are fresh, investors must pay more in fees and spread because of the lower volume and liquidity.

In several South and Middle American countries, Satoshi Tango is a direct vendor for Brazil, Chile, Colombia, Costa Rica, Ecuador, El Salvador, Guatemala, Honduras, Mexico, Nicaragua, Panama, and Peru; Bitex. la is a direct vendor for Argentina, Chile, Colombia, and Uruguay.

Local bitcoins are available on the P2P market in most Latin American countries.

MEXICO

- Gift Cards: You can purchase Bitcoin gift cards at over 5.000 stores using the Chip-Chap.com app.
- Direct: Volabit.com enables users to purchase Bitcoin with MXN through bank transfers or cash deposits at OXXO, 7-Eleven, Banamex branches, and ATMs.
- Swap: Bitso.com is a Mexican exchange. Fees are steadily decreasing as trade volume increases, to as low as 0.1 percent, and the spread is small.

BRAZIL

- Direct: Brazilians can buy Bitcoins directly at Mercadobitcoin.com.br, a broker claiming to be Latin America's largest Bitcoin exchange.
- Exchange: FlowBTC is a major Bitcoin exchange in Brazil. People can buy and sell Bitcoins here. Ban transfers may be used to make deposits. Foxbit.com.br is a second big exchange.

ARGENTINA

- Direct: Ripio is a wallet application that enables users to purchase Bitcoins. Its unique feature is that it allows you to buy Bitcoins on credit and acts as a payment gateway for Bitcoin transactions.

In Venezuela, you can buy Bitcoin.

- Bitcoin exchange: SurBitcoin is Venezuela's own Bitcoin exchange.

CHILE

- Exchange: Chile has its Bitcoin exchange, SurBTC, which

made international headlines after receiving government support. Bitcoins can be bought and sold here, and deposits in Chilean pesos can be made using local bank transfers.

EUROPE

•   ATMs: The website coinatmradar.com has a list of hundreds of Bitcoin ATMs in Europe.

•   Direct: Due to the hazy regulatory environment in the Eurozone, there is a slew of direct Bitcoin exchanges that accept a wide range of payment methods. The majority of these brokers charge their customers 0.5% to 5% fees depending on the payment channel and profit from the spread. While the sites mentioned above only sell Bitcoin and do not have an advanced online wallet, Coinbase and Circle both have an online wallet with the ability to buy Bitcoin using a bank transfer or credit card in most European countries.

•   P2P-Markets: Except for Germany, LocalBitcoin is available in every Eurozone country. Bitcoin.de is a peer-to-peer (P2P) marketplace for the entire Eurozone, where users can buy and sell Bitcoins using SEPA transfers. Except for exchanges, Bitcoin.de is the cheapest way to purchase Bitcoins, with a 0.5% commission and a low spread.

•   Exchange: Some exchanges serves the Eurozone. The most common exchange is Kraken, which Bitstamp and BTC-E follow. All exchanges require full KYC.

AUSTRIA,

Gift cards from bitcoin on. At, which are sold in several traffic shops, can be used to purchase Bitcoins by Austrian citizens. This is the most convenient but also the most expensive way of purchasing Bitcoins.

THE GERMANS

The Fidor-Bank is a good place for Germans to start buying Bitcoins. These online banks have partnered with Bitcoin.de and Kraken to make trading on these sites much quicker and easier. Fidor customers will get absolute KYC status and use the so-called ExpressTrade on Bitcoin.de right away. This allows them to purchase an infinite number of Bitcoins at low rates within minutes of contacting the website.

SPAIN

With Bit2Me.com and chip-chap.com, you can buy Bitcoins at thousands of ATMs in Spain.

EUROPE

Localbitcoins are available in almost every European country. Because of the favorable exchange rate between local currencies and the Euro, many European countries purchase Bitcoins through large European platforms (Kraken, bitcoin.de). Since high fees and widespread on small exchanges can add a significant premium to the price, it is often more cost-effective to convert the local currency to Euro and use Euro-platforms, which usually accept clients from all over Europe.

If a credit card is available, this is a convenient way to pay. Your credit card company profits from the currency exchange spread and charge; however, you can purchase Bitcoins quickly and easily.

THE UNITED KINGDOM

• Direct: U.K. residents can purchase Bitcoins directly from Coinbase using bank transfers or credit cards. Many UK residents use bittylicious.com, which, in addition to bank transfers and credit cards, provides UK-specific payment options such as Paym and Barclays Pingit. However, depending on the payment method, the fees can be very high. A third broker that provides a direct exchange is

• Exchange: Coinfloor is the most common cryptocurrency exchange in the United Kingdom, followed by Kraken and Coinbase's GDAX.

• ATM: The Swiss national railway company, SBB, recently announced that Swiss people would be able to purchase Bitcoins at every ticket machine in every rail station. Cash or electronic cash is approved as a form of payment; credit cards are not accepted. Furthermore, bitconsuisse.ch operates Bitcoin ATMs in many locations in Switzerland.

• Direct: The Bitcoinsuisse.ch broker accepts cash and bank transfers for Bitcoin purchases. 247exchange.com has added the ability to purchase Bitcoins using Franken. Other direct exchanges, such as Coinbase and Circle, welcome Swiss customers but require them to pay in Euro.

POLAND
• <u>Exchanges</u>: BitMarket.pl, BitBay.net, and bitmaszyna.pl are all good options. There are three Bitcoin exchanges in Poland where you can buy Bitcoins with Zloty at reasonable rates.

NORWAY
• <u>Direct</u>: Cubits.com allows you to buy Bitcoins directly with NOK.
• <u>Exchange</u>: There is only one exchange in Norway, bitcoinsnorway.com. However, since the price is so low, consumers must pay a premium.

SWEDEN
• <u>Direct</u>: Sweden has two Bitcoin brokers, bt.cx and fybse.se, where you can purchase Bitcoin with SEK.

DENMARK
• <u>Direct</u>: Coinify.com is the only Danish exchange.

UKRAINE
• <u>ATM</u>: Using btcu.biz, you can purchase Bitcoins from any bank ATM around the world.
• <u>Direct</u>: Buy.kuna.io provides a direct Bitcoin to Hryvna exchange. btcu.biz is another direct trade.
• <u>Exchange</u>: Ukraine now has its Bitcoin exchange, kuna.io, for Hryvna.

j NORWAY
• Direct: Cubits.com allows you to buy Bitcoins directly with NOK.
• Exchange: There is only one exchange in Norway, bitcoinsnorway.com. However, since the price is so low, consumers must pay a premium.

RUSSIA

Just a few exchanges and brokers remain in Russia due to the ambiguous legal status of Bitcoin. Localbitcoins seem to be used by a large number of people.

• Direct: matbea.com is a Bitcoin for Ruble direct seller. It necessitates the use of a phone number to register.

• BTC-E is the most popular exchange for trading Rubel and Bitcoin. It collaborates with several payment providers to allow funds to be deposited.

ASIA

Asia is the fastest-growing Bitcoin market. On exchanges in China, Japan, and South Korea, there is a brisk trade with Bitcoins, while Arabian countries like the Emirates are mostly Bitcoin-free. The best options in these countries are to locate an ATM or a seller on LocalBitcoins.

• **Exchanges in China**: China has the world's most liquid Bitcoin exchange landscape. Huobi, OKCoin, and BTC China are the exchanges with the most trading volume. Since these exchanges have no fees, the spread is extremely narrow. Aside from that, there are several other exchanges.

JAPAN

• Direct: Bitflyer.jp is the most common direct Yen, exchange broker. The broker charges very low fees and provides a wide range of verification degrees, from E-Mail to complete KYC.

• Exchange: Three exchanges serve the Japanese market: Quoine, Coincheck, and Kraken. Though they cannot compete with Chinese exchanges in terms of liquidity, they provide a decent service for purchasing Bitcoins at a low cost.

THAILAND

• Direct: bitcoin.co.th is a Bitcoin broker in Thailand. Coins.co.th, another dealer, offers a convenient online wallet.

• Exchange: Thailand now has its Bitcoin exchange, bx.in.th.

KOREA

• Direct and ATM: coinplug.com provides several options for purchasing and selling Bitcoins. They have two unique ATMs in

Seoul, allow Bitcoin purchases in thousands of ATMs across the country through a partnership with an ATM manufacturer, and offer the option to buy Bitcoins with various gift cards.

• Exchange: South Korea has a well-developed exchange, korbit.co.kr, that offers Bitcoin trading and wallets for all devices and remittance services. Coinplug.com also has an exchange.

INDIA
• Direct: Unocoin.com, India's largest Bitcoin vendor, addresses buying, selling, saving, and sending Bitcoin. Zebpay.com, another major Bitcoin platform in India, provides a similar service. These two sites, like any other exchange in India, need identity verification.

• Exchange: Coinsecure.in is a wallet and an exchange in one.

THE PHILIPPINE
In the Philippines, you can buy Bitcoins on a wide range of platforms.

• Gift cards: You can use prepaidbitcoin.ph to redeem voucher cards purchased in various locations in the Philippines.

• Direct: buybitcoin.ph is a Bitcoin and coin vendor.

• Another Ph. Coins.ph accepts various payment methods, including bank deposits, online transactions, and store coupons available nationwide.

• Exchanges: The Philippines has two Bitcoin exchanges, coinage.ph and BTCexchange.ph.

TURKEY
Although Bitcoin is not controlled in Turkey, there appears to be increasing strain on Bitcoin companies following the failed coup and increased government restrictions.

• Gift-card: Bitupcard.com allows you to purchase a Bitcoin-redeemable voucher online.

• Direct: koinim.com is a website that allows Lira users to purchase Bitcoin and Litecoin directly.

• Exchange: The first Bitcoin exchange in Turkey is BTCTurk.com. You can buy and sell Bitcoins on this site. BTCTurk recently had issues with its bank account, and there were rumors that it would have to shut down. However, it appears to be operational at this time.

MIDDLE EAST

ISRAEL
* Direct: Bits of Gold is Israel's first Bitcoin forum. You can buy and sell Bitcoins directly here.
* Bitcoin exchange: Bit2C is the largest Bitcoin exchange in Israel.
* Other: Citizens of the United Arab Emirates can buy Bitcoins directly on bitoasis.net; in Kuwait, you can buy Bitcoins on bitfils.com; in Vietnam, you can buy Bitcoins the broker bitcoinvietnam.com.vn and the exchange vbtc.vn; in Malaysia, coinbox.biz and coins.my offer an online wallet and an easy way to buy and sell Bitcoins, respectively, while oinhako.com is a wallet with the option Bitcoins can also be purchased in Indonesia at bitcoin.co.id. Taiwanese citizens can purchase, sell, and use Bitcoins on maicoin.com.

OCEANIA

AUSTRALIA
* Direct: There are many direct Bitcoin vendors in Australia: Btradeaustralia.com accepts Poli-Payments, buyabitcoin.com.au accepts cash deposits in banks, cointree.com.au accepts all payment options, coinloft.com.au accepts both payment options and Flexepin vouchers, and bitcoin.com.au allows the purchase of Bitcoin by depositing cash at kiosks.
* Exchange: Australia has two exchanges: independentreserve.com and coinspot.com.au.

NEW ZEALAND
* Direct: You can buy Bitcoins through online bank transfers at coined.co.nz and bank deposits at buybitcoin.co.nz. Coinhub.nz provides further payment options, including cash deposits at ATMs and tellers, as well as PayPal. mybitcoinsaver.com provides a wallet and the ability to invest in Bitcoins daily through automated bank transfers.
* Bitcoin exchange: There are two Bitcoin exchanges in New

Zealand. The spread on bitnz.com is reasonably broad, while nzbcx.com offers better rates.

AFRICA

In comparison to the rest of the world, Africa has a low acceptance rate for Bitcoin and just a few exchanges. In several countries, searching LocalBitcoins to find a local vendor is a good idea if no exchanges exist.

• Bit-X and ice3x.com are the two Bitcoin exchanges in South Africa (Ice Cube).

NIGERIA

• You can also exchange Bitcoins on Bit-X in Nigeria. You can also buy Bitcoins with bank transfers on nairaex.com, and buy coins with debit cards or paga on bitpesa.co.

TANZANIA

• In Tanzania, you can buy Bitcoins with bank transfers through bitpesa.co.

UGANDA

• Bitpesa.co allows Ugandans to purchase Bitcoins using MTN or Airtel Money.

ZIMBABWE

• Bitcoinfundi.com appears to be based in Zimbabwe, but the prices are shown in US dollars.

Purchasing bitcoins isn't always as easy as newcomers think. The good news is that the number of choices is growing, and it is becoming simpler.

CHAPTER 4: HOW TO CASH OUT BITCOIN: A STEP-BY-STEP GUIDE

- Do you prefer the simplest or the cheapest method?
- Do you want the funds deposited into your bank account or transferred to your PayPal account?
- How long do you want to have to wait for your money?
- What currency do you exchange your Bitcoin for?

These are some of the questions you'll have to answer for yourself. So, take a look at the methods for cashing out bitcoin mentioned below and determine which is best for you.

Exchanges of third-party brokers

An exchange is referred to as a third-party broker. Most cryptocurrency exchanges do not allow you to deposit funds with fiat currency, but a few do.

This is how it works: you deposit your Bitcoin into the exchange, then request a fiat currency withdrawal once the exchange has received your Bitcoin. A bank (wire) transfer is the most common method of doing so.

You must withdraw to the same bank account that you deposited to ensure that brokers do not violate money-laundering laws. If you've never deposited fiat on a broker exchange before, you'll almost certainly need to make (at least) one first.

I understand how irritating this can be... But that's how things are.

If you plan to cash out your Bitcoin via a broker exchange (such as Coinbase), the money will usually arrive in your account in 1-5 days. Payments are made via SEPA for EU customers (withdrawals paid in Euros). When selling Bitcoin for USD, however, brokers usually use the SWIFT payment form.

And that's how to cash out Bitcoin using a broker exchange — skip ahead to the next segment for instructions.

Let's look at how to sell Bitcoin for cash using a peer-to-peer network if you'd prefer a more anonymous and time-saving method!

Peer-to-peer (P2P)

If you don't want to wait three days to cash out your Bitcoin, a peer-to-peer selling site like LocalBitcoins could be a good option.

When selling Bitcoins to others on LocalBitcoins, you have the option of choosing which payment method the buyers can use. There are some of them:

• Cash deposit: You may request that the buyer make a cash deposit into your bank account. Before issuing your Bitcoins to them, you should always ask for proof of identification and proof of payment.

• Money Transfer: You can request a bank transfer payment from the buyer. Before attempting this method of cashing out Bitcoin, make sure to obtain proof of the buyer's identification. You can give them the Bitcoins once you've earned money.

• Meet in person for cash: You will meet with a local buyer who will pay you in cash for your Bitcoins.

If you know what you're doing, P2P selling is healthy. However, it's important to be wary of con artists. Because of their escrow service, LocalBitcoins provides a high degree of security. This locks your Bitcoins until you receive confirmation from the buyer that payment has been made.

I'm sure you're still unsure what an escrow is, so let me give you an example:

1. John wishes to purchase one Bitcoin. He looks for sellers in his own country because he is from the United Kingdom.

2. John notices that Mike is selling 1 Bitcoin for a reasonable price and allows bank transfer as a payment method.

3. John sends Mike a request for 1 Bitcoin, which he accepts.

4. Mike deposits his single Bitcoin into the escrow account. This is where John's Bitcoin is held until he transfers the funds to Mike.

5. John deposits the agreed-upon amount into Mike's account.

6. Once Mike receives the invoice, he releases the Bitcoins from the escrow and sends them to John's account.

That concludes our discussion. You now know how to trade Bitcoin for cash on a peer-to-peer (P2P) exchange.

Using a Broker Exchange to Cash Out Bitcoin

Now that you understand the differences between the two most common methods, I'll show you how to convert Bitcoins to cash using broker exchanges!

Coinbase is a cryptocurrency exchange.

The most famous broker exchange for buying and selling Bitcoin is Coinbase. They handle more Bitcoin transactions than any other broker and have a huge 13 million-strong customer base.

• Withdrawal Methods: You can exchange Bitcoins for cash on Coinbase, which you can deposit into your bank account. Only a bank account that you used to buy cryptocurrency on Coinbase can be used to cash out your Bitcoin. So, if you haven't already, I suggest starting with a small amount of cryptocurrency.

• Charges: Fees vary depending on where your bank is based. A wire transfer, for example, costs $25 if you want to exchange Bitcoin for USD. If you live in the EU and have SEPA, this will just cost you $0.15!

• Withdrawal times are also dependent on the country in which your bank is located. Withdrawals from the United States usually take 4-6 business days, although withdrawals from the European Union take 1-3 business days.

Coinbase is a service that allows you to convert Bitcoin into cash.

I'll now show you how to cash out Bitcoin at Coinbase to make things a little simpler for you.

1. You must first create a Coinbase account, connect your bank account, and make a deposit. If you need assistance, please see our guide here. If you've already completed step 1, move on to step 2!

2. After you've created your Coinbase account, send your Bitcoin to your Coinbase Bitcoin address! To do so, go to the Accounts tab and open your Bitcoin wallet before clicking "Receive." Your Bitcoin Coinbase wallet address will then be shown. This is the address to which you should submit your Bitcoin.

3. When you're ready, go to the top of the page and press

Buy/Sell.

4. Next, choose Sell.

5. The wallet is the next step in the Bitcoin cashout process. Assuming you've sent your Bitcoin to your Coinbase wallet, your Bitcoin wallet and default fiat currency should appear here. Since I opened an account in the European Union, my deposit wallet is in Euros (EUR).

6. Depending on where you are, this will change. Customers in the United States, for example, can withdraw in USD, while those in Japan can withdraw in JPY.

Your withdrawal cap will also be shown. Your limits will be very high if you have already checked your account. If you need to increase this, go to See Limits and follow the extra verification instructions!

7. You must first convert your Bitcoin to your local currency before withdrawing. In my case, I'm converting Bitcoin to Euro (EUR). Enter the sum of Bitcoin you want to sell, and the equivalent in fiat currency will be updated.

8. Your funds will now be in your fiat currency wallet after you press Sell Bitcoin Instantly.

9. Alright, we've reached the end of the process for withdrawing Bitcoin to your bank account. Click on withdraw from your fiat currency wallet (for example, EUR/USD/YEN). Your bank account information will be saved from when you first set it up. You now know how to use Coinbase to convert Bitcoin to USD, EUR, and other fiat currencies. Don't forget that there are a plethora of other brokers to choose from. Kraken is another common choice for Bitcoin sellers.

10. Another well-known exchange that accepts fiat currency deposits and withdrawals is Kraken. It's been around since 2011 and handles the majority of Bitcoin to Euro conversions. They do, however, accept other major currencies such as USD, CAD, and JPY!

• Withdrawal Methods: You can withdraw your Bitcoin to a nearby bank account if you want to convert it into cash with Kraken.

• Fees: Kraken's withdrawal fees are extremely low. A SEPA cash out, for example, costs just €0.09! It's also just $5.00 to sell Bitcoin for US dollars at a nearby US branch!

• Cash-out times: Kraken withdrawals take 1-5 business days to enter your bank account.

Using a Peer-to-Peer Exchange, convert Bitcoin to Cash

Let me show you how to cash out Bitcoin using a peer-to-peer exchange now that you know how to cash out Bitcoin using a broker. There are a few to choose from, but Local Bitcoins is the one I recommend the most.

LocalBitcoins was established in 2012 and now operates in nearly every country on the planet. So, no matter where you live, you should be able to sell your Bitcoin to buyers.

P2P has the advantage of allowing you to request any payment method you want. Here are some examples of the various payment options on LocalBitcoins:

- International Bank Wire
- Local Bank Transfer
- PayPal
- Skrill
- Payoneer
- Western Union
- Gift Vouchers
- Web Money
- Bank Cash Deposit
- Neteller

Sellers who understand how to cash out Bitcoin can also choose the price they want to sell their Bitcoin. You can do so by making an advertisement, for which you will be charged 1% of the total sale.

There are no fees if you sell to a customer who has specified the price they want to pay.

You may also leave reviews for the buyer or seller, similar to how you can on eBay. This ensures that you are protected when selecting a buyer. I just recommend selling to customers who have 100% positive reviews if you are a novice.

Local Bitcoins also allow you to remain anonymous (when using payment methods like web money or gift vouchers), especially if you protect your link with a stable and secure VPN. On the other hand, some sellers request new buyers' identification (those who have left no feedback).

Here's how to convert Bitcoin to cash using a peer-to-peer exchange, step by step:

How to Use LocalBitcoins to Cash Out Bitcoin

1. To begin, you must first create an account with Local Bitcoins. You can do so by going to this link.

2. Create a strong username and password. Your email address must also be entered and verified.

3. Once you've signed in, go to the top of the page and press Sell Bitcoins.

4. Finally, you must choose the country in which your ideal buyers are based. Of course, I suggest using your own country, but it is entirely up to you. In this case, I've chosen the United Kingdom. You'll also need to specify how much Bitcoin you want to sell.

5. As you can see, there are various ways to cash out your Bitcoin.

6. I'll show you how to cash out Bitcoin using PayPal in this example. As you can see, the buyer has a perfect rating of 100 percent and has completed over 1000 trades! This is an indication that the buyer is committed and trustworthy.

7. Enter your PayPal email address and confirm the amount of Bitcoin you want to sell. Then press the Send Trade Request button.

8. Your buyer will be notified if you want to sell your Bitcoins to them. You'll then transfer your Bitcoins to the LocalBitcoins escrow (remember how I explained an escrow earlier?). As a result, the buyer will not obtain your Bitcoins until you confirm that they have paid you.

9. You may receive notification from the buyer that the funds have been sent. Check that the funds have arrived in your PayPal account, then press Payment Received to complete the transaction.

You can practice trading using various payment methods once you've gained some experience with Local Bitcoins. The good news is that some payment methods allow you to sell your Bitcoins for a higher price, so it's worth learning how to use them.

Setting up advertising is also a smart idea. Even though it will cost you 1% in fees, you can set your price and payment process. When customers want to buy from you, you will get a notification in this situation.

LocalBitcoins is just one of many peer-to-peer exchanges that allow you to cash out your Bitcoin. The most important thing to keep in mind is that the exchange has an escrow, and you can never give your Bitcoin to a buyer until they have paid!

CHAPTER 5: GUIDE TO BUYING LITECOIN

Where to Buy Litecoin and How to Purchase Litecoin

This is largely dependent on where you are trying to buy Litecoin from and the mode of payment. This is because different 'territories' (countries and states) have different laws, and as a result, certain countries are unable to use certain Litecoin exchanges.

However, location isn't the only consideration when determining where to purchase Litecoin. There are three major factors to consider (in addition to the location/country of origin):

- Payment Method
- Country of Origin
- Fee Payments

First, consider how your payment method influences your decision...

Method of Payment

Platforms for Credit or Debit Cards

Buying Litecoin is easy, but some people can find it difficult due to how they pay for their Litecoin. Coinbase, a US-based website, allows you to buy Litecoins with a credit or debit card if you have one.

CoinMama, which is accessible from 188 countries, is another website that accepts credit cards. BitPanda, a crypto service located in the European Union, is another choice.

Platforms for Bank Transfers

BitPanda and Coinbase are two of the most user-friendly platforms for purchasing Litecoins via bank transfer.

Transfers from Coinbase will take up to five to seven working days in the United States and one to three days in the European Union. For bank transfers, Coinbase charges an average fee of 1.49 percent.

BitPanda, on the other hand, only accepts bank transfers from within the European Union.

So, if you're a US citizen looking to buy Litecoin via bank transfer, I recommend checking out Coinbase!

Before we get into the different ways you can buy Litecoins with cash or PayPal, let's talk about protection.

Never store your Litecoin on a cryptocurrency exchange (like Coinbase, Binance, etc.). Often move all of your Litecoin from your exchange to an offline wallet, a hardware wallet (like the Trezor).

Litecoin Purchases with Cash

There used to be no direct way to buy Litecoin for cash unless you met a guy down the bar who had Litecoin, and he wanted to trade his Litecoin for cash, but that doesn't sound very reliable...

Bitcoin ATMs are available, but they do not accept Litecoin. You might buy Bitcoin for cash and then exchange it for Litecoin electronically, just like many other options.

CoinFlip, on the other hand, has developed a multi-crypto ATM system that allows for Litecoin cash transactions! LTC has a cash-out feature that allows you to sell your LTC for cash.

The problem is that they're only available in the United States, and even then, there are only around thirty of them in the entire country.

Litecoins can be purchased with PayPal.

Some exchanges accept PayPal. One such platform is Cryptex24. You can choose your currency, enter the amount to be transferred, and then click "Exchange Now" to send the money, and you'll get your Litecoin within 0-4 hours of the transaction is accepted.

PayPal also made it illegal for cryptocurrency exchanges to allow the payment method. However, Cyptex24 isn't your typical exchange, and the transfer process is a good example of that.

Litecoin Purchases with Crypto

This is one of the most straightforward methods for purchasing Litecoin. If you already have Bitcoin in your wallet and have signed up, you can simply exchange LTC (Litecoin's symbol) for BTC (Bitcoin). The LTC/BTC pair is common, as is the LTC/ETH (Ether) pair!

Binance is one of the most famous and well-known cryptocurrency exchanges. In comparison to most other trading exchanges, their fees are also very modest! If you want to buy Litecoin with Bitcoin or Ethereum, this is the exchange I suggest.

Originating Country

There are federal and territorial 'locks on some sites.' Since payment methods are dependent on country-by-country partnerships, this is the case.

The easier it is to form a partnership with a country that is more "established." Coinbase is available in the United Kingdom, the United States, the European Union, Singapore, Australia, the United Arab Emirates, and Canada.

These laws are focused on exchanges that adhere to the legal requirements of local jurisdictions and countries. As a result, US customers must have different details than a German resident.

Since there is no uniform norm, exchanges must abide by the countries' electronic payment laws they wish to trade.

Charges

You should be aware of the various fees that apply and how they affect your Litecoin investments.

First and foremost, there is the miner tax. They're in Bitcoin, Ethereum, and Litecoin. This part is inevitable — regardless of which exchange you use, it will be the same.

Then there's the exchange fee to consider. Exchanges charge a commission or fee for each transaction executed on their platform in return for their services.

Comparing Litecoin Exchanges is a great way to find out where to buy Litecoin.

CoinMama, BitPanda, and Coinbase are three examples of broker exchanges (places that you can buy crypto with fiat). These are also the places to go if you want to buy Litecoin with a credit or debit card! Let's take a look at their benefits and drawbacks:

BitPanda is a cryptocurrency exchange.

The Benefits

Thanks to its compliance with EU money transfer rules, it is one of the largest brokerage crypto exchanges in the Eurozone.

Skrill, Debit and Credit Cards, Bank Giro Payments, SEPA, and other payment channels are all accepted, making purchasing Litecoin a breeze!

Disadvantages

It can only be purchased in the Eurozone.

It has an astringent verification procedure that must be followed before trading and exchanging. It has a complicated fee structure that adds to the difficulty of the experience.

Coinbase

The Benefits

Coinbase is a trading site as well as a brokerage firm. It has an excellent reputation and offers complete exchange rate services. It's extremely user-friendly!

Coinbase accepts money transfers and credit/debit card payments as payment types.

Disadvantages

Unlike other sites that cover 100+ countries, Coinbase is only available in 33 countries. Coinbase isn't available in every country.

Furthermore, Coinbase's verification tests are extremely stringent! The ID tests you complete determine your account limits.

CoinMama

The Benefits

CoinMama accepts a wide range of payment methods, including debit and credit cards, Western Union, and MoneyGram. This ensures that people who don't have access to conventional banking will use the portal.

The platform is available in every country and can be accessed from anywhere! Verification is, therefore, less of an issue than for other suppliers.

Disadvantages

CoinMama's fees are higher than those of other vendors, and it does not offer Litecoin. The main problem with CoinMama is that it does not allow bank transfers.

Many exchanges, like CoinMama, will not let you buy Litecoin. Instead, you'll need to purchase a different cryptocurrency (such as Bitcoin or Ether) and then pass it to a trading exchange to purchase Litecoin.

Let's take a look at each phase of the process to see how to buy Litecoin on some of the most common platforms.

Coinbase is the best place to buy Litecoin.

Coinbase allows you to buy Litecoin with your fiat currency (USD, EUR, etc.). Let's get started! It's beginner-friendly, so let's get started!

The first step is to create a Coinbase account, which you can do on your computer or by downloading the Coinbase app from the App Store (iOS) or Play Store (Android) (Android).

Your Coinbase account can be linked to your bank account, credit card, or even debit card.

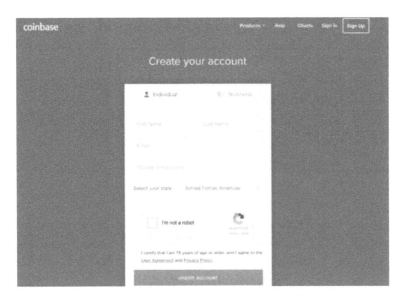

You'll need to double-check if they're your bank accounts or credit cards. After you've completed these steps, you'll be able to buy (and sell) Litecoin.

The next step is to purchase Litecoin.

On your Android or Apple smartphone, open the app. Scroll down to Litecoin on the homepage. Select the graph by clicking on it. You'll be taken to the next screen.

Owing to security restrictions, screenshots are not permitted on the next two windows. But it's very easy. The graph is on the next page, and below it are two blue buttons that say buy and sell. Select 'purchase' from the drop-down menu.

When you get to the buy tab, you can choose your payment method and the amount of fiat you want to spend. After that, you can purchase Litecoin.

It's as simple as that on Coinbase!

BitPanda is a great place to buy Litecoin.

BitPanda allows you to purchase Litecoin. The first move is to create a BitPanda account, which you can do by downloading the BitPanda app from the Apple App Store or Google Play. This will provide you with a secure method of purchasing Litecoin. To set up your account and buy your first Litecoin, follow these measures.

You will need to create an account. To create a simple account, you'll need to follow the on-screen instructions.

BitPanda requires all users to register to comply with Eurozone regulations. There are three stages, each of which has a time limit. The most expensive choice is Gold Verification, but it removes account limits.

For this method to function, you'll need your identification documents and access to a webcam.

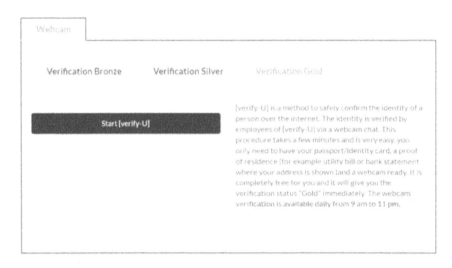

You'll have full access to your trading account once you've registered and checked your account. Your starting point is the home screen (shown above).

Let's go ahead and buy some Litecoin on BitPanda.

You can now buy Litecoin with the funds you want to add from your EUR/LTC wallet transaction after you've selected Litecoin from the cryptocurrencies.

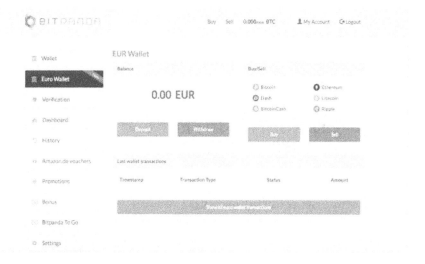

The processing time can also differ depending on the degree of account verification (so bear that in mind).

Purchasing Litecoin on BitPanda is as easy as that!

CHAPTER 6: THE DIFFERENCE BETWEEN BITCOIN AND LITECOIN

A Comparison of Bitcoin and Litecoin

The public's interest in cryptocurrencies has shifted dramatically over the last few years. Investor interest in cryptos has risen dramatically since the turn of the century. The main subject of this attention has been Bitcoin, which has long been the most well-known brand in cryptocurrencies, unsurprising. It was the first digital currency to gain widespread acceptance.

Hundreds of other cryptocurrencies have entered the market since the launch of Bitcoin in 2009.1 While it has become increasingly difficult for digital coins to stand out in such a crowded field, Litecoin (LTC) is one non-Bitcoin cryptocurrency that has managed to hold its own. LTC is currently the sixth-largest digital currency by market capitalization, trailing only Bitcoin.

- Bitcoin and Litecoin are both digital currencies. Bitcoin, which was established in 2009, is the most famous cryptocurrency; Litecoin, which was founded two years later, is one of its main competitors.

- Bitcoin's market cap is $1 trillion as of March 2021, while Litecoin's is $13.7 billion.2

- Litecoin can produce more coins and has a faster transaction speed than Bitcoin. These are primarily psychological benefits for investors and have no bearing on the currency's value or usability.

- Bitcoin and Litecoin use cryptographic algorithms fundamentally different: Bitcoin uses the longstanding SHA-256 algorithm, while Litecoin uses the newer Scrypt algorithm.
Bitcoin and Litecoin have a lot in common.

On the surface, Bitcoin and Litecoin appear to be very similar. They are both decentralized cryptocurrencies at their most basic stage. Unlike fiat currencies like the US dollar or the Japanese yen, which depend on central banks for value, circulation control, and legitimacy, cryptocurrencies are decentralized. They rely solely on the network's cryptographic integrity for value, circulation control, and legitimacy.

Litecoin was founded in 2011 by former Google engineer Charlie Lee, who announced the launch of the "lite version of Bitcoin" via a message on a prominent Bitcoin forum. Litecoin was seen as a reaction to Bitcoin from the start. Indeed, Litecoin's creators have claimed for years that their goal is to build the "silver" to Bitcoin's "gold."

As a result, Litecoin adopts many of the features of Bitcoin that Lee and other developers thought were useful in the earlier cryptocurrency while also changing certain elements that the development team thought could be enhanced.

Work Samples

The fact that both Bitcoin and Litecoin are proof of work ecosystems is a significant similarity. That is to say, the process by which both cryptocurrencies are mined—that is, created, authenticated, and then added to a public ledger or blockchain—is fundamentally the same.

Transactions and Storage

Many of the essential elements of transacting with Bitcoin and Litecoin are also very similar for an investor. Both of these cryptocurrencies can be purchased on a cryptocurrency exchange or mined with a mining rig. To be safely stored between transactions, both require a digital or cold storage "wallet."

Furthermore, the values of both cryptocurrencies were shown to be highly volatile over time, depending on a variety of factors such as investor interest and government regulations.

Bitcoin vs. Litecoin: What's the Difference?

Capitalization of the market

The market capitalization, or total dollar market value of all outstanding coins, is one region where Bitcoin and Litecoin vary significantly.

The total amount of all bitcoins in existence is about $1 trillion as of March 2021, making Bitcoin's market cap more than 70 times that of Litecoin, which has a total value of $13.7 billion.2 If you consider Bitcoin's market cap to be big or low depends mostly on your historical context. When we remember that the market capitalization of Bitcoin was just $42,000 in July 2010, the current figure seems incredible.

Bitcoin also outnumbers all other digital currencies as a network. Given that Bitcoin is so far larger than all other digital currencies in existence at this moment, its closest rival is Ethereum, the second-largest cryptocurrency, with a market cap of approximately $212 billion.2 Therefore, the fact that Bitcoin has a considerably higher valuation than Litecoin is not surprising.

Distribution

Another significant distinction between Bitcoin and Litecoin is the total amount of coins that each cryptocurrency produces. This is where Litecoin sets itself apart. The Bitcoin network will never hold more than 21 million coins, while the Litecoin network can hold up to 84 million.

While this appears to be a major benefit for Litecoin in principle, its real-world implications may be minor. This is because both Bitcoin and Litecoin can be divided into almost infinitesimal numbers. The smallest amount of Bitcoin that can be transferred is one hundred millionth of a bitcoin (0.00000001 bitcoins), also known as one "satoshi."

Regardless of how high the general price of an undivided single Bitcoin or Litecoin rises, users of either currency should have no trouble buying low-cost products or services.

Litecoin's greater number of maximum coins could give a psychological advantage over Bitcoin due to the lower price for a single unit.

In November 2013, IBM executive Richard Brown raised the

possibility that some users may prefer transacting in whole units rather than in fractions of a unit, a possible benefit for Litecoin.5 But even assuming this is true, the problem may be solved by simple software changes implemented in the digital wallets through which Bitcoin transactions are made.

As Tristan Winters points out in a Bitcoin Magazine post, "The Psychology of Decimals," common Bitcoin wallets such as Coinbase and Trezor now provide the option to show the Bitcoin value in terms of official (or fiat) currencies such as the U.S. dollar. This can help circumvent the psychological aversion to dealing with infractions.

Transaction Speed

While theoretically, transactions occur instantaneously on both the Bitcoin and Litecoin networks, time is taken to validate such transactions by other network participants. Litecoin was developed to prioritize transaction speed, and that has proven an asset as it has increased in popularity.

According to information from Blockchain.com, the Bitcoin network's average transaction confirmation period (the time it takes for a block to be validated and added to the blockchain) is currently just under nine minutes per transaction. However, this can vary widely when traffic is high. The equivalent figure for Litecoin is approximately 2.5 minutes.

In theory, this difference in confirmation time may make Litecoin more appealing for merchants. For example, a vendor selling a product in exchange for Bitcoin will need to wait nearly four times as long to validate the payment as if the same product were sold in exchange for Litecoin. Merchants, on the other hand, can also accept transactions without waiting for any confirmation. The security of zero-confirmation transactions is a hot topic of discussion.

Transaction Speed

While transactions on the Bitcoin and Litecoin networks are theoretically instantaneous, it takes time for those transactions to be validated by other network participants. Litecoin was created to prioritize transaction speed, which has proven to benefit as the currency has increased in popularity.

According to Blockchain.com, the average transaction confirmation period (the time it takes for a block to be checked and added to the blockchain) on the Bitcoin network is currently under nine minutes per transaction. However, this can vary greatly when traffic is high. Litecoin's equivalent figure is approximately 2.5 minutes.

This difference in confirmation time might, in theory, make Litecoin more appealing to merchants. A retailer selling a product in exchange for Bitcoin, for example, will have to wait nearly four times as long to receive a payment confirmation as if the same product was sold in exchange for Litecoin. On the other hand, merchants can often choose to approve transactions without waiting for confirmation. The safety of zero-confirmation transactions is a point of contention.

Algorithms.

The use of different cryptographic algorithms is by far the most fundamental technical discrepancy between Bitcoin and Litecoin. The long-standing SHA-256 algorithm is used by Bitcoin, while Scrypt is a relatively new algorithm used by Litecoin.

The effect of these various algorithms on the method of mining new coins is their most functional significance. Confirming transactions in both Bitcoin and Litecoin necessitates a significant amount of computing resources. Miners are members of the currency network who devote their computational power to verifying other users' transactions. These miners are compensated for their efforts by receiving units of the currency they have mined.

SHA-256 is a more complicated algorithm than Scrypt, but it allows for more parallel processing. As a result, Bitcoin miners have become increasingly advanced in recent years to mine bitcoins as efficiently as possible. The use of Application-Specific Integrated Circuits (ASICs) is the most popular approach for Bitcoin mining.

Unlike the basic CPUs and GPUs that came before them, these are hardware systems customized to mine Bitcoins. As a result, Bitcoin mining has become completely out of reach for the average person unless they enter a mining pool.

Scrypt, on the other hand, was created to be less vulnerable to the custom hardware solutions used in ASIC-based mining. Many observers believe that Scrypt-based cryptocurrencies like Litecoin are more open to users who also want to participate in the network as miners. Although some companies have released Scrypt ASICs,

Litecoin's vision of more easily accessible mining remains a reality, as the majority of Litecoin mining is still performed on miners' CPUs or GPUs.11

LITECOIN VS. BITCOIN FAQS

What Is Litecoin Used For?

Given the uproar surrounding its prices and market capitalization, Litecoin may exist primarily to be bought and sold, to paraphrase an old traders' joke about soybeans. However, Litecoin, like all cryptocurrencies, is a form of digital currency. Individuals and organizations may use it to make purchases and move funds between accounts.

It's suitable for smaller, daily transactions because of its relative speed and low cost. Without using an intermediary such as a bank, credit card business, or payment processing service, participants work directly.

Can You Convert Litecoin to Bitcoin?

You can swap litecoins for bitcoins and vice versa, just as you can do with fiat currencies like dollars for pounds or yen for euros. Swapping one for the other is usually not a concern since they are both leading and extremely liquid cryptocurrencies.

To do so, you'll need a cryptocurrency trading or exchange network or trading app account. The amount you'll get from the conversion is, of course, determined by the current exchange rates for and currency.

Is it possible to submit Litecoin to a Bitcoin wallet?

Since you can't submit Litecoin to a Bitcoin address (even though they're in the same wallet), it's crucial to recognize cryptocurrency conversion. You will lose money if you do so. If you have seed backups for the keys that allow you to access your account, recovery can be possible, but it's difficult.

Is Litecoin on the verge of displacing Bitcoin?

It's anyone's guess if Litecoin would ever surpass Bitcoin as the most famous cryptocurrency. Bitcoin is the first digital currency, and many people associate it with cryptocurrencies in general—almost it's a generic word like Kleenex is for facial tissue.

If any other cryptocurrency were to dethrone Bitcoin, Ethereum (currently ranked second) or one of the other higher-ranked currencies would be the most probable candidates. Litecoin's fundamentals, however, are liked by some analysts. In a 2018 article for The Motley Fool, stock picker Sean Williams wrote, "Litecoin can process transactions faster than bitcoin, and its faster block time means that it can handle more power than bitcoin," adding, "it most certainly has the tools to drive bitcoin aside and become the go-to medium of exchange for digital currency users."

Although Bitcoin and Litecoin are currently the gold and silver of the cryptocurrency space, history has shown that the status quo in this fast-moving and still-developing industry will shift in a matter of months. It's unclear if the cryptocurrencies we've become acquainted with will maintain their prominence in the months and years ahead.

You may have heard the word "blockchain," the record-keeping technology behind the Bitcoin network, whether you've been following finance, trading, or cryptocurrencies over the last ten years.

- A blockchain database is a special kind of database.
- The storage method varies from that of a traditional database; blockchains store data in blocks that are then chained together.
- As new information is received, it is entered into a new block. If the block has been filled with data, it is chained onto the previous block, resulting in a chronological chain of data.
- A blockchain can store various data, but the most popular use has been as a transaction ledger.
- In the case of Bitcoin, blockchain is used in a decentralized manner, meaning that no one individual or community has power—rather, all users have control collectively.
- Decentralized blockchains are permanent, meaning the data entered cannot be changed. This ensures that transactions in Bitcoin are permanently registered and accessible to everyone.

<u>What is Blockchain?</u>
While blockchain appears to be complicated, and it can be, its core concept is rather easy. A database, or blockchain, is a form of digital ledger. To comprehend blockchain, it is essential to first comprehend

what a database is.

A database is a collection of data stored on a computer device in an electronic format. Database information, or data, is usually organized in table format to make searching and filtering specific information easier.

What's the difference between a spreadsheet and a database when it comes to storing data?

Spreadsheets are structured to store and access limited quantities of data for a single individual or a small group of people. On the other hand, a database is structured to hold much greater volumes of data that can be accessed, filtered, and manipulated by any number of users at the same time.

Large databases do this by storing information on servers comprised of powerful computers. To provide the computing power and storage space required for multiple users to access the database simultaneously, these servers may often be constructed using hundreds or thousands of computers. Although anyone can access a spreadsheet or database, a company is often owned and maintained by a designated person who has full control over its functions and the data it contains.

So, what's the difference between a blockchain and a database?

Storage Structure

The way data is structured significantly between a traditional database and a blockchain. A blockchain is a digital ledger that organizes data into groups called blocks, each containing a collection of data. When a block is filled, it is chained onto the previous filled block, creating a " blockchain "data chain." All new knowledge that comes after the newly added block is compiled into a newly created block, added to the chain until it is filled.

A database organizes information into tables, while a blockchain organizes information into chunks (blocks) linked together. Both blockchains are databases as a result, but not all databases are blockchains. When applied in a decentralized manner, this system creates an irreversible data timeline. When a block is filled, it becomes permanent and part of the timeline. When a block is attached to the chain, it is assigned an exact timestamp.

Attributes of Cryptocurrency

Decentralization

It's helpful to think about blockchain in terms and how it's been applied by Bitcoin to better understand it. Bitcoin, like a database, relies on a network of computers to store the blockchain. This blockchain is simply a form of the ledger that records every Bitcoin transaction ever made for Bitcoin. In the case of Bitcoin, unlike most databases, these machines are not all housed under one roof, and each computer or group of computers is run by a single person or group of people.

Consider a corporation that maintains a server with 10,000 computers and a database that contains all of its clients' account records. This organization owns a warehouse that houses all of these computers under one roof and has complete control over them and the information they hold. Similarly, Bitcoin is made up of thousands of computers. Still, each computer or group of computers that holds its blockchain is located in a different part of the world and is run by different people. Nodes are the machines that make up the Bitcoin network.

The blockchain of Bitcoin is used in a decentralized manner in this model. On the other hand, private, centralized blockchains exist in which all of the machines that make up the network are owned and run by a single individual.

Each node in a blockchain has a complete record of all data stored on the blockchain since its inception. The data for Bitcoin is the complete history of all Bitcoin transactions. If a node's data contains an error, it may use the thousands of other nodes as a point of reference to fix it. This way, no single node in the network can change the data it contains. As a result, the past transactions in each block of Bitcoin's blockchain are unchangeable.

If one user tampers with Bitcoin's transaction record, all other nodes can cross-reference each other, making it easy to find the node that has the incorrect data. This method aids in the establishment of a precise and straightforward sequence of events. A blockchain can store various information, such as legal contracts, state identifications, or a company's product inventory. For Bitcoin, this information is a list of transactions, but it can also contain various information, such as legal contracts, state identifications, or a company's product inventory.

The majority of the decentralized network's computing power will have to agree on the changes to alter how the system operates or the information stored inside it. This means that any improvements that do take place are in the majority's best interests.

Transparency

Due to Bitcoin's decentralized nature, all transactions can be transparently viewed using a personal node or blockchain explorers, which enable everyone to see transactions as they happen in real-time. Every node has a copy of the chain that is updated as new blocks are added and checked. This means that if you wanted to, you could follow Bitcoin wherever it goes.

Exchanges, for example, have been compromised in the past, resulting in the loss of all Bitcoin stored on the exchange. Although the hacker can remain unidentified, the Bitcoins they stole are easily traceable. It would be known if the Bitcoins stolen in any of these hacks were transferred or spent somewhere.

Is Blockchain a Safe Investment?

In many ways, blockchain technology addresses the issues of protection and trust. First and foremost, new blocks are often stored in sequential and chronological order. That is, they are often added to the blockchain's "top." If you look at the Bitcoin blockchain, you'll notice that each block has a spot on the chain called a "height," which had reached 656,197 blocks as of November 2020.

It is difficult to go back and change the contents of a block after it has been added to the end of the blockchain unless the majority agrees. Each block has its hash and the hash of the block before it and the time stamp listed earlier. A math function converts digital data into a string of numbers and letters, resulting in hash codes. The hash code changes if the information is changed in some way.

Here's why that matters in terms of protection. Let's say a hacker tries to change the blockchain to steal Bitcoin from the rest of the world. If they changed their single copy, it would no longer match the copy of anyone else. When anyone else compares their versions, they'll notice that this one stands out, and the hacker's version of the chain will be discarded as illegitimate.

To succeed in such a hack, the hacker will have to simultaneously manipulate and change 51 percent of the blockchain copies, ensuring that their new copy becomes the majority copy and, therefore, the agreed-upon chain. An attack like this would cost a lot of money and energy because they'd have to redo all of the blocks. After all, the timestamps and hash codes would be different now.

The cost of pulling off such a feat will almost certainly be impossible, given Bitcoin's network's scale and how quickly it is increasing. This would not only be prohibitively costly, but it would also be futile. Such actions would not go unnoticed by network members, who would note such significant changes to the blockchain. Members of the network will then fork off to a new, unaffected version of the chain.

This would cause the value of the attacked version of Bitcoin to plunge, rendering the attack futile since the bad actor would have a worthless asset. If a malicious guy attacked Bitcoin's latest fork, the same thing would happen. It's designed this way so that participating in the network is much more financially rewarding than targeting it.

BLOCKCHAIN VS. BITCOIN

Blockchain aims to allow for the recording and distribution of digital data without editing it. Stuart Haber and W. Edwards first proposed blockchain technology in 1991. Scott Stornetta, two researchers, tried to build a method that could not be tampered with when it came to recording timestamps. Blockchain didn't have its first real-world implementation until almost two decades later, with the introduction of Bitcoin in January 2009.

A blockchain is the foundation of the Bitcoin protocol. Bitcoin's pseudonymous founder, Satoshi Nakamoto, described the digital currency as "a new electronic cash system that's completely peer-to-peer, with no trusted third party" in a research paper introducing it.

The important thing to remember is that Bitcoin only uses blockchain to create a transparent ledger of payments; however, blockchain can theoretically be used to immutably record any number of data points. As previously stated, this may take the form of purchases, election votes, commodity inventories, state identifications, home deeds, and much more.

Currently, there are a plethora of blockchain-based ventures attempting to use blockchain for purposes other than transaction documentation. The use of blockchain as a voting system in democratic elections is a clear example. Because of the immutability of blockchain, fraudulent voting will become even more difficult.

For example, a voting scheme may be set up such that each resident of a country receives a single cryptocurrency or token. Each candidate would then be assigned a unique wallet address, and voters would send their tokens or crypto to the address of the candidate they wish to support. Since blockchain is transparent and traceable, it eliminates the need for human vote counting and bad actors' potential to tamper with physical ballots.

BANKS VS. BLOCKCHAIN

Decentralized blockchains and banks are vastly different. Let's equate the banking structure to Bitcoin's blockchain implementation to see if it varies from the blockchain.

What is the Role of Blockchain?
Blocks on Bitcoin's blockchain, as we now know, store data about monetary transactions. However, it turns out that blockchain can also store data about other forms of transactions.

Walmart, Pfizer, AIG, Siemens, Unilever, and many other firms have also adopted blockchain technology. IBM, for example, has developed the Food Trust blockchain1 to monitor the path that food items take to reach their destinations.

Why are you doing this? Countless outbreaks of E. coli, salmonella, and listeria, as well as toxic chemicals inadvertently added to foods, have occurred in the food industry. It used to take weeks to figure out what was causing these outbreaks or what was causing people to get sick from what they were eating.

Brands can monitor a food product's journey from its origin to each stop it makes, and finally to its distribution, thanks to blockchain. If a food is found to be infected, it can be traced back to its source by each stop. Not only that, but these firms will now see what else they've come into contact with, potentially saving lives and allowing the issue to be identified much earlier. This is one example of a blockchain in action, but there are several other ways to incorporate a blockchain.

Banking and financial services

Banking is perhaps the industry that stands to gain the most from incorporating blockchain into its business operations. Financial institutions are only open five days a week during business hours. That means that if you want to deposit a check at 6 p.m. on Friday, you'll probably have to wait until Monday morning to see the funds in your account. Even if you make your deposit during business hours, it can take one to three days for the transaction to be verified due to the high volume of transactions that banks must process. Blockchain, on the other hand, is awake all the time.

Consumers can see their transactions completed in as little as ten minutes2 by incorporating blockchain into banks, which is the time it takes to add a block to the blockchain, regardless of holidays or the time of day or week. Banks can now exchange funds between institutions more easily and safely, thanks to blockchain. The settlement and clearing process in the stock market industry, for example, can take up to three days (or longer if trading internationally), which means that the money and shares are frozen during that time.

Because of the large amounts involved, even a few days in transit will result in substantial costs and banks' risks. According to the European bank Santander and its research partners, the potential savings range from $15 billion to $20 billion per year3. Capgemini, a French consultancy, estimates that blockchain-based technologies could save customers up to $16 billion per year4 in banking and insurance fees.

Currency

Blockchain is the foundation for cryptocurrencies like Bitcoin. The Federal Reserve is in control of the US dollar. A user's data and currency are legally at the discretion of their bank or government under this central authority scheme. If a user's bank is compromised, their personal information is exposed. The value of a client's currency may be jeopardized if their bank fails or if they reside in a country with an authoritarian government. Some of the banks that went bankrupt in 2008 were partly bailed out with taxpayer money. These are the concerns that led to the creation and development of Bitcoin.

Blockchain enables other cryptocurrencies to function without a central authority's need by distributing their activities through a network of computers. This not only lowers risk but also removes a lot of the transaction and processing costs. It can also provide a more secure currency with more applications and a larger network of individuals and institutions to do business, both domestically and internationally, for countries with unstable currencies or financial infrastructures.

For those who do not have state identification, using cryptocurrency wallets for savings accounts or as a means of payment is particularly important. Some countries may be in the midst of a civil war, or their governments may lack the necessary infrastructure to provide identification. Citizens of such countries may be unable to open savings or brokerage accounts, leaving them with no means of securely storing money.

Health-care

Health-care providers may use blockchain to store their patients' medical records safely. When a medical record is created and authenticated, it can be stored on the blockchain, giving patients evidence and assurance that the record cannot be altered. These personal health records could be encrypted and stored on the blockchain with a private key, meaning that only certain people can access them.

Records of Property

If you've ever visited your local Recorder's Office, you know how slow and time-consuming the process of recording property rights can be. A physical deed must now be sent to a government employee at the local recording office, who manually enters it into the county's central database and public index. Land arguments must be reconciled with the public index in the event of a property dispute.

This procedure is not only expensive and time-consuming, but it is also prone to human error, with each inaccuracy reducing the efficiency of property ownership monitoring. Scanning records and tracking down physical files in a local recording office may be obsolete thanks to blockchain. Property owners can assume that their deed is valid and permanently registered if stored and validated on the blockchain.

It can be virtually impossible to prove ownership of a property in war-torn countries or places with little or no government or financial infrastructure and no "Recorder's Office." Land ownership timelines might be defined straightforwardly and consistently if a group of people residing in such an area could use blockchain.

Smart Contracts

A smart contract is a computer code embedded in the blockchain to help promote, check, or negotiate a contract. Users agree to a set of conditions for smart contracts to work. The terms of the agreement are immediately carried out until those conditions are met.

Let's say a prospective tenant wants to lease an apartment using a smart contract. When the occupant pays the security deposit, the landlord offers to give the apartment's door code tenant. Both the tenant and the landlord must send their portions of the agreement to the smart contract, which would keep track of the door co code and automatically swap it for the security deposit on the lease's start date. The security deposit is refunded if the landlord fails to include the door code by the lease date. This will remove the costs and procedures associated with using a notary, third-party mediator, or attorneys.

Chains of Distribution

Suppliers may use blockchain to track the source of materials they buy, similar to the IBM Food Trust example. Along with popular labels like "Organic," "Local," and "Fair Trade," this will enable businesses to check the authenticity of their goods.

According to Forbes, the food industry is increasingly using blockchain to monitor the direction and protection of food during the farm-to-user journey.

Voting

As previously mentioned, blockchain could be used to aid in the creation of a modern voting system. As shown in the November 2018 midterm elections in West Virginia, voting with blockchain can reduce electoral fraud and increase voter turnout. Using blockchain in this way would make tampering with votes nearly impossible. The blockchain protocol will also ensure democratic accountability by reducing the number of people required to run an election and providing officials with near-instant results. There would be no need for recounts, and there would be no real risk that the result would be tainted by fraud.

THE BENEFITS AND DRAWBACKS OF BLOCKCHAIN

Despite its difficulty, blockchain's ability as a decentralized record-keeping system is almost limitless. Blockchain technology can have applications beyond those mentioned above, ranging from increased user privacy and protection to lower transaction fees and fewer errors. However, there are several drawbacks.

Advantages
- Increased precision by eliminating the need for human verification.
- Cost savings by obviating the need for third-party verification
- Decentralization makes it more difficult to tamper with data.
- Transactions are safe, convenient, and fast.
- Transparent hardware
- Provides residents of countries with insecure or underdeveloped governments with a banking option and a way to protect personal details.

Drawbacks
- Bitcoin mining has a significant technological expense.
- Transactions per second are low
- Use of illegal acts in the past
- Legislation

Benefits of Blockchain
Transaction Accuracy on the Blockchain A network of thousands of computers approves transactions on the blockchain network. This virtually eliminates human intervention in the verification process, resulting in lower human error and a more reliable data record. And if one of the computers on the network made a cryptographic error, it would only affect one copy of the blockchain. To spread to the rest of the blockchain, the mistake will have to be made by at least 51 percent of the network's computers, which is nearly impossible in a massive and network like Bitcoin's.

Reduced Costs

Consumers typically pay a bank to validate a transaction, a notary to sign a document or a minister to marry them. The blockchain removes the need for third-party authentication, as well as the costs that come with it. When businesses accept credit card payments, they must pay a small fee to banks and payment processing firms to process the transactions. On the other hand, Bitcoin has no central authority and only has a small transaction fee.

Blockchain doesn't keep all of its data in a single location. Instead, a network of computers copies and spreads the blockchain. Every device on the network updates its blockchain to represent a new block to the blockchain. Blockchain makes it more difficult to tamper with data by disseminating it through a network rather than storing it in a single central database. If a hacker obtained a snapshot of the blockchain, only a single copy of the data would be compromised rather than the entire network.

Transactions that are quick and easy

The settlement of transactions made through a central authority will take several days. For example, if you deposit a check on Friday evening, you can not see your account's funds until Monday morning. Blockchain operates seven days a week, 24 hours a day, and 365 days a year, while financial institutions operate during business hours, five days a week. Transactions can be done in as little as ten minutes, and after just a few hours, they are considered stable. This is especially useful for cross-border transactions, which take much longer due to time zone differences and the requirement that both parties confirm payment processing.

Transactions in Confidentiality

Many blockchain networks function as public databases, allowing anyone with an internet connection to access the network's transaction history. While users have access to transaction data, they do not have access to identifying information about the users who are conducting the transactions. It's a common misconception that blockchain networks like bitcoin are private when they're not.

Rather than their details, a user's unique code, known as a public key, is stored on the blockchain when making public transactions. A person's identity is always connected to their blockchain address if they made a Bitcoin purchase on an exchange that needs authentication. However, even when bound to a person's name, a transaction may not disclose personal details.

Secure Transactions

The blockchain network must verify the validity of a transaction after it has been registered. Thousands of computers on the blockchain scramble to verify that the purchase's details are right. The transaction is applied to the blockchain block after a device has checked it. The blockchain has its unique hash, as well as the hash of the previous block. The hashcode of a block changes when the information on it is changed somehow; however, the block's hashcode after it does not. Because of this disparity, changing details on the blockchain without warning is extremely difficult.

Transparency is essential.

The majority of blockchains are made up entirely of open-source software. This ensures that anyone with access to the internet can look at the code. This allows auditors to check the security of cryptocurrencies, including Bitcoin. This also implies that no real authority exists on who owns Bitcoin's code or how it is edited. As a result, everyone can propose system improvements or adjustments. Bitcoin will be upgraded if most network users accept that the latest version of the code with the upgrade is sound and worthwhile.

Banking the Unbanked

The ability for anybody, regardless of race, gender, or cultural context, to use blockchain and Bitcoin is perhaps its most significant feature. According to World Bank, nearly 2 billion adults lack bank accounts or other means of holding their money or assets. 5 Almost all of these people live in developing countries, where the economy is still in its infancy and money is king.

These individuals also receive small amounts of money that are paid in cash. They must then hide this physical cash in their homes or business places, leaving them vulnerable to theft or needless abuse. A bitcoin wallet's keys can be written down, saved on a cheap mobile phone, or even memorized if necessary. These solutions are more likely to be hidden than a small cash pile under a mattress for most people.

Blockchains of the future are also searching for ways to store medical records, property rights, and a host of other legal contracts in addition to being a unit of account for wealth storage.

Blockchain's Disadvantages

While the blockchain has many benefits, it also has many drawbacks when it comes to adoption. Today's roadblocks to blockchain technology adoption aren't only technological. For the most part, the real obstacles are political and legislative, not to mention the thousands of hours (read: money) of custom software design and back-end programming needed to incorporate blockchain into existing business networks. The following are some of the roadblocks to widespread blockchain adoption.

Technology Cost

Although blockchain can save users money on transaction fees, it is not a free technology. Bitcoin's "proof of work" scheme, for example, consumes a tremendous amount of computing resources to verify transactions. In the real world, the power generated by the bitcoin network's millions of computers is roughly equivalent to Denmark's annual electricity consumption. Mining costs, except hardware costs, are about $5,000$7,000 per coin, assuming $0.03$0.05 per kilowatt-hour energy costs.

Despite the high costs of bitcoin mining, consumers continue to increase their energy bills to validate blockchain transactions. That's because miners are compensated with enough bitcoin for their time and effort when adding a block to the bitcoin blockchain. However, miners will need to be charged or otherwise incentivized to verify transactions on blockchains that do not use cryptocurrencies.

Some solutions to these problems are starting to emerge. Bitcoin mining farms, for example, have been set up to use solar power, waste natural gas from fracking sites, or wind farm power.

Speed Inefficiency

Bitcoin is an excellent example of blockchain's potential inefficiencies. It takes about ten minutes for Bitcoin's "proof of work" method to add a new block to the blockchain. According to estimates (TPS), the blockchain network can only handle about seven transactions per second at that point. Other cryptocurrencies, such as Ethereum, outperform bitcoin, but they are still constrained by blockchain. For background, the legacy Visa brand can process 24,000 TPS.

For years, people have been working on solutions to this issue. Some blockchains can handle over 30,000 transactions per second right now.

Illegal Behavior

While the blockchain network's anonymity protects users from hacking and maintains their privacy, it also allows for illicit trade and operation. The Silk Road, an anonymous "dark web" drug marketplace that operated from February 2011 until October 2013, when the FBI shut it down, is perhaps the most well-known example of blockchain being used for illegal transactions.

Users may search the website without being monitored and make illegal Bitcoin and other cryptocurrency purchases using the Tor browser. According to current US regulations, financial service providers must collect information about their customers before they open an account, check each customer's identity, and ensure that customers do not appear on any list of confirmed or alleged terrorist groups. This method has both advantages and disadvantages. It helps everyone to access financial accounts, but it also makes it easier for criminals to transact. Many have argued that the positive uses of cryptocurrency, such as banking the unbanked, outweigh the negative uses, particularly because most criminal activity is still carried out with untraceable cash.

Regulation

Many people in the crypto community are worried about government oversight of cryptocurrencies. Governments could potentially make it illegal to own cryptocurrencies or participate in their networks, despite ending anything like Bitcoin is becoming extremely difficult and nearly impossible as its decentralized network develops.

As large corporations like PayPal continue to promote the ownership and usage of cryptocurrencies on their platforms, this issue has diminished.

What Does the Future Hold for Blockchain?

Blockchain, which was first proposed as a research project in 19917, is now in its late twenties. Blockchain, like most millennials its generation, has gotten a lot of press in the last two decades, with companies all over the world speculating about what the technology will do and where it will go in the future.

With many practical applications for the technology already being applied and explored, blockchain, at the age of twenty-seven, is gradually making a name for itself, thanks in no small part to bitcoin and cryptocurrencies. Blockchain, a buzzword on the lips of any investor in the country, promises to make business and government operations more accurate, reliable, stable and cost-effective by eliminating middlemen.

It is no longer a question of "whether" legacy businesses would adopt blockchain—it's a question of "when." As we enter the third decade of blockchain, it's no longer a question of "if."

CHAPTER 7: BITCOIN MINING

What is Bitcoin Mining?

Cryptocurrency mining is time-consuming, costly, and only lucrative on rare occasions. On the other hand, many cryptocurrency investors are drawn to mining because miners are compensated with crypto tokens in exchange for their efforts. This may be because, like California gold prospectors in 1849, entrepreneurs regard mining as a divine gift. If you are technologically inclined, why not try it?

However, before you invest your time and money into mining, read this explanation to see if it's right for you. We'll concentrate on Bitcoin (we'll use "Bitcoin" to refer to the network or cryptocurrency as a term throughout, and "bitcoin" to refer to several individual tokens).

- You will raise cryptocurrency without having to pay for it through mining.
- Bitcoin miners are paid in Bitcoin to complete "blocks" of validated transactions and add them to the blockchain.
- The miner who discovers a solution to a complex hashing puzzle first receives a reward. The likelihood that a participant will be the one to discover the solution is proportional to their share of the network's overall mining capacity.
- To set up a mining rig, you will need either a GPU (graphics processing unit) or an application-specific integrated circuit (ASIC).

A New Gold Rush

The promise of being paid with Bitcoin is a major draw for many miners. To be clear, you do not need to be a miner to own cryptocurrency tokens. You can purchase cryptocurrencies with fiat currency, swap them on an exchange like Bitstamp with another cryptocurrency (for example, Ethereum or NEO to buy Bitcoin), or gain them by shopping, writing blog posts on sites that pay users in cryptocurrency or even setting up interest-earning crypto accounts. Steemit is an example of a crypto blog site similar to Medium but allows users to reward bloggers with STEEM, a proprietary cryptocurrency. STEEM can then be exchanged for Bitcoin elsewhere.

Miners receive a Bitcoin reward as an incentive to help with mining's primary goal, legitimizing and tracking Bitcoin transactions to ensure their validity. Bitcoin is a "decentralized" cryptocurrency, meaning it is not regulated by a central authority such as a central bank or government, so these obligations are distributed to several users worldwide.

HOW TO MINE BITCOINS

Auditor miners are compensated for their efforts. They are in charge of ensuring that Bitcoin transactions are legitimate. Satoshi Nakamoto, the inventor of Bitcoin, devised this convention to keep Bitcoin users truthful. Miners help to avoid the "double-spending crisis" by checking transactions.

Double spending refers to a scenario in which a bitcoin owner spends the same bitcoin twice. This isn't an issue with real money: if you send someone a $20 bill to buy a bottle of vodka, you don't have it anymore, so there's no chance of them using it to buy lottery tickets next door. While counterfeit money is a possibility, spending the same dollar twice is not. According to the Investopedia dictionary, "there is a risk that the holder will make a copy of the digital token and give it to a merchant or another party while holding the original."

Assume you have one $20 bill that is authentic and one $20 bill that is counterfeit. If you tried to spend both the genuine and false bills, anyone who looked at the serial numbers on both of them would find that they were identical, meaning that one of them was fake. A Bitcoin miner operates similarly, reviewing transactions to make sure users aren't spending the same bitcoin twice. As we'll see further down, this isn't a true analogy.

After checking 1 MB (megabyte) worth of bitcoin transactions, known as a "block," miners are entitled to be rewarded with bitcoin. Satoshi Nakamoto set the 1 MB limit, a contention source among miners, who believe the block size should be increased to accommodate more data, allowing the bitcoin network to process and verify transactions more quickly.

Note that a coin miner will receive bitcoin after verifying 1 MB of transactions; however, not everyone who verifies transactions will be paid out.

1MB of transactions can potentially be as little as one (though this is extremely rare) or as many as several thousand. It is dependent on the amount of data consumed by the transactions.

"So, even after all that work of checking transactions, I might not get any bitcoin in return?"

Yes, you are right.

To gain bitcoins, you must fulfill two requirements. One is a result of commitment, and the other is a result of chance.
1) You must check approximately 1MB of transactions. This is the most straightforward element.
2) You must be the first miner to solve a numerical problem with the correct answer or the nearest answer. Evidence of work is another name for this procedure.

"What exactly do you mean when you say 'the correct answer to a numeric problem'?"

The good news is that no advanced mathematics or computation is needed. Miners aren't supposed to solve difficult mathematical problems, but that isn't the case. They're attempting to be the first miner to generate a 64-digit hexadecimal number (a "hash") that is either less than or equal to the target hash. It's essentially a guessing game.

The bad news is that its guesswork, but with the total number of potential guesses for each of these problems in the trillions, it's extremely taxing. Miners need a lot of computational power to solve a problem first. You'll need a high "hash rate" to mine successfully, which is calculated in megahashes per second (MH/s), gigahashes per second (GH/s), and terahashes per second (TH/s).

There are a lot of hashes there.

Cryptocompare provides a useful calculator for estimating how much bitcoin you might mine with your mining rig's hash rate.

Bitcoin mining and circulation

Mining serves another important function besides lining miners' pockets and maintaining the bitcoin ecosystem: it is the only way to release new cryptocurrencies into circulation. To put it another way, miners are essentially "minting" money. For example, there were approximately 18.5 million bitcoins in circulation as of November 2020. Miners were responsible for producing any single Bitcoin, except the coins minted by the genesis block (the first block, which Satoshi Nakamoto created). In the absence of miners, the Bitcoin network will continue to run and be usable. However, no new bitcoin will be produced. Bitcoin mining will end at some point, with the total number of bitcoins capped at 21 million according to the Bitcoin Protocol. However, since the rate at which bitcoins are "mined" slows over time, the final bitcoin won't be distributed until about 2140. This isn't to assume that all transactions will be scrutinized. Miners will have to verify transactions and be rewarded for their contributions to preserve the Bitcoin network's credibility.

Coin mining will grant you "voting" control when changes to the Bitcoin network protocol are proposed, in addition to the short-term Bitcoin payoff. To put it another way, miners have a say in how forking decisions are made.

HOW MUCH DOES A MINER MAKE?

Every four years, the incentives for bitcoin mining are halved. One block of bitcoin was worth 50 BTC when it was first mined in 2009. This was reduced to 25 BTC in 2012. By 2016, it had been cut in half again, to 12.5 BTC. The reward was halved again on May 11, 2020, to 6.25 BTC. November of 2020, the price of Bitcoin was about $17,900 per Bitcoin, which meant that completing a block would earn you $111,875 (6.25 x 17,900). 3 It does not seem to be a bad incentive to solve the complex hash problem mentioned above.

You may consult the Bitcoin Clock, which updates this information in real-time, to keep track of when these halvings will occur. Interestingly, bitcoin's market price has continued to correlate strongly with the reduction of new coins entering circulation over its existence. Because of the lower inflation rate, the shortage has increased, and prices have risen in response.

If you're curious about how many blocks have been mined so far, many websites, including Blockchain.info, will provide you with that information in real-time.

Is There Anything I Need To Mine Bitcoins?

People may have been able to compete for blocks with a standard at-home machine early on in Bitcoin's history, but this is no longer the case. This is because the complexity of mining Bitcoin fluctuates over time. The Bitcoin network aims to generate one block every 10 minutes to ensure the blockchain's smooth operation and ability to process and validate transactions. However, if one million mining rigs compete to solve the hash problem, they would most likely find a solution faster than ten mining rigs work on the same problem. As a result, every 2,016 blocks, or approximately every two weeks, Bitcoin evaluates and adjusts mining complexity. As more computing power is pooled to mine Bitcoin, the difficulty level of mining rises to maintain a consistent block production rate. The complexity level decreases as computing power decreases. To give you an idea of how much computational power is involved, consider that when Bitcoin first released in 2009, the difficulty level was one. It is more than 13 trillion dollars as of November 2019.

All of this means that miners must now invest in powerful computer equipment such as a GPU (graphics processing unit) or, more realistically, an application-specific integrated circuit to mine competitively (ASIC). These can cost anything from $500 to tens of thousands of dollars. Individual graphics cards (GPUs) are purchased by some miners, especially Ethereum miners, as a low-cost way to put together mining operations.

THE "EXPLAIN IT LIKE I'M FIVE" VERSION

The ins and outs of bitcoin mining are complicated enough as it is. Consider the following illustration of how the hash problem works: I tell three friends I'm thinking of a number between one and one hundred, and I write it down on a piece of paper and enclose it in an envelope. My friends do not have to guess the exact number; all they have to do is be the first to guess any number that is less than or equal to the one I'm considering. There is no limit on the number of guesses they will get.

Let's pretend I'm considering the number 19. They lose if Friend A guesses 21 because 21>19. Instead of 1619 and 1219, if Friend B guesses 16 and Friend C guesses 12, they've both technically arrived at viable answers. Even though Friend B's response was closer to the mark of 19, there is no "extra credit" for him. Consider the following scenario: I ask three friends to guess what number I'm thinking of, but I'm not thinking of a number between 1 and 100. Rather, I'm pondering a 64-digit hexadecimal number and asking millions of would-be miners. You can see how difficult it would be to guess the correct answer.

If B and C both respond at the same time, the ELI5 analogy fails.

Simultaneous responses are popular in Bitcoin, but there can only be one winning response at the end of the day. When multiple simultaneous responses are equal to or less than the target number, the Bitcoin network will choose which miner to honor based on a simple majority—51 percent. Typically, the miner who has completed the most work or verified the most transactions is the winner. After that, the losing block is referred to as an "orphan block." The term "orphan block" refers to a block that has not been added to the blockchain. Miners who have solved the hash problem but haven't checked the most transactions aren't paid in bitcoin.

What Does It Mean to Have a "64-Digit Hexadecimal Number"?

Here's an example of a number like this:
0000000000000000057fcc708cf0130d95e27c5819203e9f967ac56e4df598ee

The above number has 64 digits. So far, it's been fairly simple to comprehend. As you might have noted, the number includes both numbers and letters from the alphabet. What is the reason for this?

Let's unpack the term "hexadecimal" to see what these letters are doing in the middle of numbers.

As you might be aware, we use the "decimal" scheme based on base ten. As a result, each digit of a multi-digit number has ten possibilities, ranging from zero to nine.

"Hexadecimal," on the other hand, refers to the base 16 system, as "hex" comes from the Greek word for six and "deca" comes from the Greek word for ten. Each digit in the hexadecimal system has 16 possible values. However, our numerical method only provides ten different ways to represent numbers (zero through nine). That is why you must insert letters, namely letters a, b, c, d, e, and f.

You don't need to calculate the total value of that 64-digit number if you're mining bitcoin (the hash). You don't need to measure a hash's total worth, I repeat.

So, what exactly are "64-digit hexadecimal numbers," and how do they relate to bitcoin mining?

Remember how I wrote the number 19 on a piece of paper and sealed it in an envelope for the ELI5 analogy?

The goal hash is the unknown metaphorical amount in the envelope in bitcoin mining terms.

Miners are guessing at the goal hash with those massive computers and thousands of cooling fans. Miners make these guesses by making as many "nonces" as they can as quickly as they can. The secret to creating these 64-bit hexadecimal numbers I keep talking about is a nonce, which stands for "number only used once." A nonce in Bitcoin mining is 32 bits long, much smaller than the hash, 256 bits. The first miner to produce a hash that is less than or equal to the goal hash is credited with completing the block and receives 6.25 BTC as a reward.

You could theoretically obtain the same result by rolling a 16-sided die 64 times to generate random numbers, but why would you want to?

"How do I figure out what the goal hash is?"

All target hashes start with zeros, with a minimum of eight and a maximum of 63 zeros.

There is no minimum target, but the Bitcoin Protocol has set a maximum target. No goal can be higher than this:

00000000ffff0000000000000000000000000000000000000000000000000000

00000000

Here are some examples of randomized hashes, as well as the requirements for determining whether they can contribute to miner success:

"How can I improve my odds of guessing the goal hash before someone else?"

You'd need to invest in a powerful mining rig or, more realistically, enter a mining pool, which is a collection of coin miners who pool their computing power and divide the bitcoin they mine. Mining pools are similar to Powerball teams, in which members purchase lottery tickets in bulk and plan to split the proceeds. Pools mine a relatively large number of blocks compared to individual miners.

To put it another way, it's purely a numbers game. You can't make a prediction based on previous target hashes or guess the pattern. At the time of writing, the most recent block's difficulty level is about 17.59 trillion, which means that every given nonce has a one in 17.59 trillion chance of generating a hash below the mark. Even with a super-powerful mining rig, you don't stand a chance if you're operating alone.

"How do I know if bitcoin is going to be successful for me?"

Miners must not only consider the costs of the costly equipment used to solve a hash problem. They must also know how much electricity mining rigs can generate massive amounts of nonces to pursue the solution. As of this writing, bitcoin mining is essentially unprofitable for most individual miners. Cryptocompare has a handy calculator where you can type in numbers like the hash and energy costs to estimate the costs and benefits.

WHAT ARE COIN MINING POOLS AND HOW DO THEY WORK?

The miner who discovers a solution to the puzzle first receives mining rewards. The probability that a participant will be the first to discover the solution is proportional to their share of the network's total mining power. Individuals with a small percentage of the mining power have a very slim chance of independently discovering the next block. For example, a mining card costing a couple of thousand dollars would represent less than 0.001% of the network's total mining power. With such a small chance of finding the next block, it could take a long time for that miner to find one, and as the difficulty increases, things become even more difficult. The miner's investment can never be recouped. Mining pools are the solution to this issue. Third-party mining pools manage and organize groups of miners. Miners can get a steady flow of bitcoin from the day they activate their miner by working together in a pool and sharing payouts among all participants. Blockchain.info has statistics on a few of the mining pools.

"I've crunched the numbers. Don't bother with mining. Is there a less time-consuming way to make money with cryptocurrencies?"

As previously stated, the simplest way to obtain bitcoin is to purchase it on one of the numerous exchanges. You may also use the "pickaxe technique" as an alternative. This is based on the adage that during the 1849 California gold rush, the smart investment was to make mining pickaxes rather than pan for gold. Alternatively, invest in the companies that make those pickaxes in today's terms. A company that manufactures Bitcoin mining equipment would be the pickaxe equivalent in the cryptocurrency world. Instead, you could look into companies that manufacture ASICs or GPUs, for example.

Is Bitcoin Mining a Legitimate Business?

The legality of Bitcoin mining is entirely dependent on your location. The concept of Bitcoin may pose a threat to fiat currency dominance and government control of financial markets. As a result, Bitcoin is completely illegal in some jurisdictions.

Bitcoin mining and ownership are legal in a growing number of countries. Algeria, Egypt, Bolivia, Morocco, Ecuador, Nepal, and Pakistan are just a few examples of countries where it is prohibited. 4 Overall, Bitcoin mining and use are legal in most parts of the world.

Risks of Mining

The risks associated with mining are frequently financial and regulatory. Mining, in general, is a financial risk, as previously stated. One could go to great lengths to purchase mining equipment worth hundreds or thousands of dollars only to see no return on their investment. However, by entering mining pools, this risk can be reduced. If you're thinking about mining but live in a region where it's forbidden, you should think twice. It is also a great idea to look into your country's cryptocurrency regulations and sentiment before purchasing mining equipment.

Another possible risk associated with the rise of bitcoin mining (and other proof-of-work schemes) is the increased energy consumption of the computer systems that run the mining algorithms. Although the performance of ASIC chips has improved significantly, the network's growth is outpacing technological advancement. As a result, there are questions about Bitcoin mining's environmental effects and carbon footprint. There are, however, attempts to reduce this negative externality by using carbon offset credits and finding safer and greener energy sources for mining operations (such as geothermal or solar). Another tactic is to switch to less energy-intensive consensus mechanisms like proof-of-stake (PoS), which Ethereum plans to do. However, PoS has its collection of disadvantages and inefficiencies

CONCLUSION

For the past two years, Bitcoin has been firmly in the media spotlight. Even if Bitcoin is no longer relevant, cryptocurrencies have shown viable alternatives to institutionally backed internet transactions.

The number of daily Bitcoin transactions has increased this month. Over the short term, the number of transactions has risen while the price of Bitcoin has remained relatively stable, suggesting stable growth patterns. Still, bullish Bitcoin analysts are few and far between. Mastercard announced that it regards all anonymous Bitcoin transactions as "suspicious transactions," giving the technology an unavoidably dark impression.

Federal law enforcement agencies continue to be concerned about criminal activity and the use of Bitcoin in black markets on the "Deep Web." Bitcoin's success and anonymity make it a desirable option for criminals who depended solely on cash and unruly banks. When developed with a political agenda, technological innovations have appeared to be libertarian; most new applications and software developments have bolstered Bitcoin's anonymizing capabilities (Dark Wallet is the primary example). Tech advancements will continue to affect the government's ability to control Bitcoin and other virtual currencies, influencing potential policy decisions.

Although many people sought bitcoin currency to circumvent government regulation, the high rate of illegal activity via Bitcoin rendered regulation inevitable. In the last two years, the US government has accepted Bitcoin as a form of property and started to regulate it. By registering businesses that use Bitcoins, the government hopes to make illegal activity involving the currency more difficult.

CPSIA information can be obtained
at www.ICGtesting.com
Printed in the USA
BVHW091130150621
609530BV00011B/2102